Pennsylvania
CIVIL WAR TRAILS

Pennsylvania
CIVIL WAR
TRAILS

THE GUIDE TO BATTLE SITES, MONUMENTS, MUSEUMS AND TOWNS

TOM HUNTINGTON

STACKPOLE BOOKS

Pennsylvania
Historical & Museum
Commission

Published by
STACKPOLE BOOKS
5067 Ritter Road
Mechanicsburg, PA 17055
www.stackpolebooks.com

Printed in the United States of America

10 9 8 7 6 5 4 3 2 1

FIRST EDITION

Design by Beth Oberholtzer
Cover design by Caroline Stover

Photographs by the author unless otherwise noted

Cover: **Officers of the 3rd Pennsylvania Cavalry in 1862.** LIBRARY OF CONGRESS

Library of Congress Cataloging-in-Publication Data

Huntington, Tom.
    Pennsylvania Civil War trails : the guide to battle sites, monuments, museums, and towns / Tom Huntington.
       p.   cm.
    Includes bibliographical references.
    ISBN-13: 978-0-8117-3379-3 (pbk.)
    ISBN-10: 0-8117-3379-3 (pbk.)
    1. Pennsylvania—History—Civil War, 1861–1865—Campaigns. 2. Trails—Pennsylvania—Guidebooks. 3. Historic sites—Pennsylvania—Guidebooks. 4. Pennsylvania—Tours. 5. Pennsylvania—History—Civil War, 1861–1865—Battlefields—Guidebooks. 6. United States—History—Civil War, 1861–1865—Battlefields—Guidebooks. 7. United States—History—Civil War, 1861–1865—Campaigns. I. Title.

E527.H865   2007
973.709748—dc22

                                        2006029702

Contents

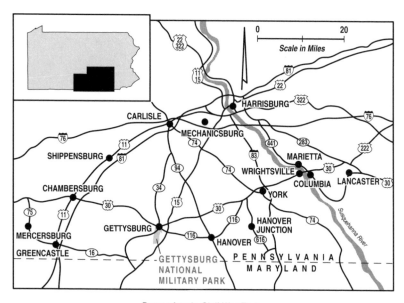

Pennsylvania Civil War Trails

Preface

"The past is never dead," said novelist William Faulkner. "It's not even past."

That's certainly true along Pennsylvania's Civil War Trails, seven itineraries that help travelers discover Civil War history for themselves throughout the state's south-central portion. The routes pass down country roads that once reverberated with the hoofbeats of Confederate cavalry, through small towns that witnessed the march of armies, and to various museums and buildings that tell their own stories of the time when war came to Pennsylvania. Parts of the trails seem as though they've hardly changed at all, and travelers pass by many of the same barns, farmhouses, and fields that the Confederates under Gen. Robert E. Lee would have seen. Other portions have undeniably surrendered to the modern world, and it requires an effort of the imagination to block out the strip malls, gas stations, cars, and highways and imagine what things must have been like in 1863.

The trails' centerpiece is Gettysburg, the National Military Park in Adams County where a Union army under Maj. Gen. George Gordon Meade defeated Lee and his Army of Northern Virginia in July 1863. The three-day battle marked a definite turning point in the war, and ended Lee's ambitious invasion of Pennsylvania. Yet Gettysburg provides only a portion of Pennsylvania's Civil War history, one piece of the full story. Taken together, the communities along the Civil War trails create a rich mosaic. They tell the stories, not just of the fighting men who took up arms for the Union, but also of the civilians—men and women, white and black—who suddenly found war on their doorsteps.

Introduction
The Stage Is Set

Pennsylvania was indeed a keystone state for the Union cause. When the Civil War broke out with the bombardment of Fort Sumter in April 1861, the Federal army was woefully unprepared. It had a mere 16,000 men under arms. Many of those, including some of its finest officers, cast their allegiance with the South. President Abraham Lincoln quickly put out a call for 75,000 volunteer soldiers to serve for ninety days. That was the most the president could request without an act of Congress, and Congress was not in session.

Even before the attack on Sumter, Pennsylvania Governor Andrew Gregg Curtin had taken steps to revitalize the state's militia. Born in 1815 in Bellefonte, Curtin attended law school at Dickinson College in Carlisle and appeared destined for great things. He was elected governor in 1860 as a Republican—the party of Lincoln, whose own election sparked the secession of Southern states—and he realized that war was inevitable. After meeting with the president in Washington four days before

Pennsylvania governor Andrew Gregg Curtin was a staunch ally of President Abraham Lincoln. LIBRARY OF CONGRESS

the Fort Sumter attack, Curtin hurried home and asked the legislature to take steps to strengthen the state's military preparedness. When war did come, Pennsylvania sent the first units to defend the nation's capital. Five companies of men left the Harrisburg train station on April 18, bound for Washington. They had no weapons and little training, but Lincoln greeted these "First Defenders" with a great sense of relief and sent them to guard the Capitol building. By the end of the war, Pennsylvania had contributed 215 regiments, independent batteries, emergency militia, and U.S. Colored Troops and provided for around 427,000 enlistments.

Although Pennsylvania contributed mightily to the war effort with men and supplies, by late spring 1863 the state had been largely untouched by the conflict. War had come close in September 1862 when armies clashed at the Battle of Antietam in nearby Sharpsburg, Maryland, and it had even briefly lapped over the border, when Confederate cavalry under Maj. Gen. J. E. B. "Jeb" Stuart raided as far north as Chambersburg that October. In the late spring of 1863, residents in the farmlands and small towns in Pennsylvania near the Mason-Dixon line had real cause for concern. It appeared that an enemy army was poised to invade their land.

The threatening force was the Confederate Army of Northern Virginia, Gen. Robert E. Lee commanding. In May, Lee's forces had handed the Union the latest in a long series of embarrassments at the Battle of Chancellorsville. The battle had started well for the Union. Maj. Gen. Joseph E. Hooker, commanding the Army of the Potomac, crossed the Rappahannock River and moved efficiently to threaten the Southern army's flank and rear. Then Hooker, perhaps too aware of how often Lee had outfoxed the Union, apparently lost his nerve. Instead of continuing his offensive, he settled into a defensive position and waited for Lee to attack him.

Lee was more than happy to oblige, even though he was outnumbered. In defiance of traditional military thinking, Lee divided his forces in the face of superior numbers, and sent Lt. Gen. Thomas J. "Stonewall" Jackson with 30,000 men on a circuitous, seventeen-mile march that brought him to the unsuspecting enemy's right flank. There, as day faded into twilight, Jackson's men fell on the Union's XI Corps in a brilliant surprise attack that sent the Union right reeling. Had darkness not fallen, it could have been a complete rout. Instead, the attack turned

Gen. Robert E. Lee decided to bring the war north into Pennsylvania in 1863. LIBRARY OF CONGRESS

into a tragedy for the South. Jackson rode forward in advance of his own lines to reconnoiter, and his own men shot him as he rode back. Mortally wounded, Stonewall Jackson died days later.

Lee's army won the field at Chancellorsville, but its losses were severe. With Jackson, Lee had lost his "right arm." Worse yet, his already battered army suffered an additional 12,000 men killed, wounded, or captured. Lee threw the Union army back across the Rappahannack, but he gained no ground. Union forces still threatened the Confederate capital of Richmond. The Southern troops still needed food and forage for their horses, items in short supply in war-ravaged northern Virginia. After Chancellorsville, Lee saw that he had two options—either retire to Richmond and "stand a siege, which must ultimately have ended in surrender, or to invade Pennsylvania."

Heading north had other things in its favor. A successful campaign on the enemy's soil might force the Union to consider peace, or persuade European powers to intercede on the Confederacy's side. It might even force the Federals to divert forces from the western theater of operations and reduce pressure on the Mississippi city of Vicksburg, then being squeezed by the Union army under Maj. Gen. Ulysses S. Grant.

Lee was not the kind of general who inclined to the defensive. He decided to head north to Pennsylvania.

Lee first reorganized his army from two into three corps, plus a cavalry division. The I Corps remained under Lt. Gen. James Longstreet. Stolid and deliberate in battle, the general from Georgia was a dependable commander whom Lee referred to as his "old warhorse." Longstreet's I Corps had three divisions, under Maj. Gens. Lafayette McLaws, George E. Pickett, and John Bell Hood.

Jackson had commanded Lee's II Corps. To replace his "right arm," Lee picked Lt. Gen. Richard S. Ewell, known as "Old Bald Head" for reasons obvious to anyone who sees his portrait. The eccentric Ewell was a peppery, blunt-spoken soldier with an admirable command of profanity.

Lt. Gen. Richard S. Ewell replaced Stonewall Jackson as commander of Lee's II Corps. LIBRARY OF CONGRESS

Brig. Gen. John B. Gordon said that Ewell "had in many respects the most unique personality I have ever known. He was a compound of anomalies, the oddest, most eccentric genius in the Confederate army." Born in Washington, D.C., and raised in Virginia, Ewell had graduated from West Point in 1840, trained at Carlisle Barracks in Pennsylvania, and fought in Mexico. As an engineer, he had done survey work in southern Pennsylvania, experience that would prove helpful in the summer of 1863.

Ewell lost a leg in August 1862 at the Battle of Groveton, the opening act in Second Manassas. When he returned to the Army of Northern Virginia to take command of the II Corps, he had a wooden leg and a new bride, a widow he had married three days before assuming his new command. He still referred to her as "Mrs. Brown." According to rumors, he had promised her he would curb his profanity.

Ewell's three divisions were commanded by Maj. Gens. Jubal A. Early, Robert E. Rodes, and Edward "Allegheny" Johnson, also known as "Clubby" because of the stick he used as a cane following a wound he received in the Shenandoah Valley. Early was another of the South's eccentrics, an abrasive and hard-drinking character who would continue to fight the Civil War on paper long after it ended on the battlefield. Ewell and his men would make themselves known, and occasionally notorious, throughout much of central Pennsylvania.

Lee put his newly created III Corps in the hands of Maj. Gen. Ambrose Powell Hill, who had gained a reputation as a dependable fighter under Stonewall Jackson. Hill's three divisions were commanded by Maj. Gens. Richard H. Anderson, Henry Heth, and William D. Pender.

A vitally important part of Lee's army was the cavalry division under the command of Maj. Gen. James Ewell Brown "Jeb" Stuart, one of the legendary fighting figures of the Civil War. Dashing, daring, and skillful,

Stuart led a cavalry that could ride circles around the Union, sometimes literally. During the Peninsula Campaign outside Richmond, Stuart embarrassed the Federals and their commander, Maj. Gen. George B. McClellan, by taking his cavalry all the way around them. With his long beard, plumed hat, and cocky, confident air, Stuart created the very picture of a dashing Southern cavalier.

The Virginia-born Stuart also had a long relationship with Robert E. Lee, who had been superintendent at West Point when Stuart entered the military school as a cadet in 1850. In 1859, when abolitionist John Brown made his raid on Harpers Ferry, Virginia, in a doomed attempt to spark a slave insurrection, Lee commanded the detachment of Marines who captured him. The man Lee sent forward to negotiate when Brown holed up in a fortified firehouse in Harpers Ferry was Stuart. He had just happened to be in Washington, trying to sell the army a saber grip he had developed, when the crisis arose, and he quickly volunteered to help Lee subdue Brown and his men.

In spring 1863, Lee intended his invasion to be a huge foraging mission, and Pennsylvania farmers throughout the region would soon bemoan the loss of crops, horses, cows, and pretty much anything that wasn't nailed down. But Lee did not want to spark widespread resentment against his army, so he forbade plundering and wanton destruction in his General Order No. 72. Not that Confederates didn't take what they needed, but when they did pay, it was usually with useless Confederate money. "We shall get nearly a million dollars worth of horses and supplies of all kinds from Franklin County alone, and we have also invaded Fulton and Adams Counties, and shall levy on them in like manner," noted Robert E. Lee's mapmaker, Jedediah Hotchkiss. "We are supporting the army entirely on the enemy."

When Lee moved his army into Pennsylvania, it appeared that he would once again face Joseph

Pennsylvanians grew to fear Confederate cavalry commander Maj. Gen. J. E. B. Stuart, who raided the state in 1862 and returned a year later for Lee's Gettysburg campaign.

Hooker and the Army of the Potomac, the force he had defeated at Chancellorsville. Hooker's army, though, was roiled by in-fighting, probably because it had tasted more defeat than victory in its brief history.

The first major battle between Union and Confederate armies had taken place in July 1861, when the Rebels sent the Federals under Brig. Gen. Irvin McDowell reeling back to Washington, D.C., after the first Battle of Manassas (also called Bull Run). President Abraham Lincoln responded by replacing McDowell with Philadelphia native George B. McClellan, "the Young Napoleon." McClellan was as certain of his abilities as he was unwilling to commit his forces, and his reluctance to grapple with his foes continually frustrated the civilian authorities in Washington. He finally launched an ambitious effort to take the Confederate capital of Richmond, but Robert E. Lee's superior generalship forced McClellan into retreat during the Seven Days' Battles on the Peninsula in the spring of 1862.

Lincoln next placed the Union's eastern fortunes in the hands of Maj. Gen. John Pope, who was soundly whipped by Lee at Second Manassas (or Second Bull Run) in August 1862. It didn't help that some Union officers were content to see Pope lose, provided that his defeat meant McClellan's return. With no other options at hand, Lincoln reappointed McClellan to command a unified Army of the Potomac.

Lee planned to take the war north and invade Maryland. In September 1862, the cautious McClellan was spurred into action after a Union soldier found a copy of Lee's orders to his army wrapped around some cigars and dropped in a field. McClellan now knew Lee's plans, and he made his move. The two armies crashed together on the banks of Antietam Creek near the town of Sharpsburg, Maryland, on September 17, 1862. The fighting was hot and furious. More than 23,000 soldiers fell that day, either dead or wounded. It was the bloodiest single day in American history.

Although the fighting had been pretty much a draw, Lee withdrew his force back across the Potomac River and into Virginia. McClellan did not follow. Lincoln, frustrated by this general and his "case of the slows," replaced him with Maj. Gen. Ambrose Burnside. The new commander was a big, strapping man with elaborate whiskers that gave birth to the word "sideburns," but he was, by his own estimation, a poor general. He demonstrated the accuracy of his self-assessment at the Battle of Fredericksburg in December 1862, when he sent his soldiers on a hopeless attack against Lee, safely ensconced on the high ground behind the town.

Burnside's defeat meant a new commander for the Army of the Potomac. Joe Hooker was a competent commander, but a man whose own hubris—and skill at criticizing his superiors—widened the divisions among his officers. Hooker had done what he could to plant his knives in Burnside's back. After Chancellorsville, the daggers were aimed squarely at his own. One officer, Maj. Gen. Darius N. Couch, was so disgusted with Hooker that he asked to be transferred. He ended up in Harrisburg as the commander of the Department of the Susquehanna, newly formed to defend central Pennsylvania.

Lee began moving his army of about 75,000 men north in early June. His first target was a small force under Maj. Gen. Robert Milroy in Winchester, Virginia, at the northern end of the Shenandoah Valley. The Shenandoah, bounded by the long ridges of the Allegheny Mountains to the west and the Blue Ridge Mountains to the east, pointed like a broad avenue toward the heart of Pennsylvania, and it also provided a fine route toward Washington. As a result, the valley had long been an object of much attention from North and South.

Milroy stubbornly remained in Winchester despite increasing pressure from Washington to withdraw. Finally, on June 13, soldiers in Early's division attacked. Milroy attempted to retreat early on the morning of June 15, but the Confederates routed his forces, capturing 3,400 men and killing or wounding 1,000. The remainder fled, and it wasn't long before the men and wagons of Milroy's shattered command were streaming northward into Pennsylvania.

Hooker began moving his army north to shadow Lee, always keeping it between the Confederates and Washington, D.C, but "Fighting Joe" lost his chance for a rematch. His missteps, strained rela-

Gen. George G. Meade accepted command of the Army of the Potomac with reluctance, only days before the clash at Gettysburg. LIBRARY OF CONGRESS

tionships with his subordinates, and even more strained relationship with Henry Halleck, general-in-chief of the Union armies, finally forced his resignation.

Hooker's replacement was one of his corps commanders, a no-nonsense Pennsylvanian named George Gordon Meade. Born in Cadiz, Spain, to American parents, Meade had grown up in Philadelphia and graduated from West Point in 1831. He fought bravely in Mexico and had proven himself a dependable and aggressive, if sometimes hot-tempered, commander on the field. Balding, beaky, and with big pouches under his eyes that gave him an air of melancholy, Meade was "a damned old goggle-eyed snapping turtle," as one of his soldiers described him, but he was no prima donna. He had not sought command of the Army of the Potomac, but he nonetheless received his orders to take command early in the morning on June 28. He was still getting the feel for his army as it pursued Robert E. Lee into Pennsylvania. On June 30 he wrote his wife, "I am going straight at them, and will settle this thing once and for all."

Franklin County
The Invasion Begins

Greencastle

Zip along U.S. Route 11 just north of Greencastle, Pennsylvania, and you might miss the granite obelisk that stands alongside the road in front of a white farmhouse. Below the obelisk lie the remains of Corp. William Rihl, the first Union soldier killed in action in Pennsylvania. It was a distinction Rihl probably would have happily declined had he been given the chance.

Rihl was a gardener in Philadelphia when he joined the 1st New York (Lincoln) Cavalry in 1861 to fight for the Union. Two years later, on June 22, 1863, Confederate cavalrymen under Brig. Gen. Albert Jenkins ambushed Rihl and other members of his unit here on a farm owned by the Fleming family. A Confederate bullet struck Rihl in the head and killed him instantly on the spot where the obelisk stands. He was only twenty.

The Confederates buried Rihl in a shallow grave, but Greencastle residents dug him up for reburial in the town's Lutheran cemetery. In 1886 they moved Rihl back to the place where he died and the state of Pennsylvania raised this obelisk to honor "an humble but brave defender of the Union." Except for Route 11's asphalt ribbon and the traffic that whooshes along it, things haven't changed much here since Rihl had his date with destiny. The Fleming farm remains in the hands of Fleming

The Rihl Monument in Greencastle honors the first Union soldier killed in action above the Mason-Dixon line, Corp. William Rihl.

descendents, and the tang of manure from the surrounding fields indicates the presence of farmland.

Greencastle lies just a mile or so to the south. The Mason-Dixon line, the boundary between Pennsylvania and Maryland that once separated slaveholding territory from free soil, lies just a few miles beyond that. When the Civil War erupted in 1861, Greencastle was a quiet town of about 1,300 people, clustered around a central square called the Diamond. Greencastle's a little bigger now, but the Diamond remains, although it's now a traffic rotary. Just around the corner is the former McCullough's Tavern, where George Washington supposedly breakfasted on October 13, 1794, as he headed west to deal with the Whiskey Rebellion. The building has since been converted into a laundromat, but if you peer through a hole in the fence between it and the adjoining pizza joint, you can spot some of the original log construction.

The Whiskey Rebellion never reached Greencastle, and for a time residents didn't think the Civil War would either. "The secessionists of Virginia will never get north of the Potomac," the Reverend Edwin Emerson wrote to a friend eleven days after Confederate guns fired on Fort Sumter. Emerson was a pastor who had left Greencastle to teach at Troy University and later served as an emissary to England and France. He expressed his zeal for the Union by writing "Death to traitors" at the top of his letter.

Emerson's epistle is one of many in a box of Civil War correspondence at Greencastle's Allison-Antrim Museum, a small history collection housed in a Civil War–era building. Its storage room is a small upstairs room, which is stuffed with boxes and lined with shelves of objects related to local history.

 Greencastle

Incorporated in 1995, The **Allison-Antrim Museum**, 365 S. Ridge Ave., includes a number of Civil War relics. Its building was constructed in 1860 by local hardware store owner Alexander L. Irwin. The museum is open on the second Sunday of each month from 1 PM to 4 PM, and one Thursday each month from noon to 3 PM (717) 597-9010, www.greencastlemuseum.org. The **Rihl Monument** is north of Route 16 on Route 11.

One box contains an entire collection of black-bordered *Philadelphia Inquirers* that detail Lincoln's assassination and funeral, and the hunt for "the dastard assassin." A high beaver hat sits on a plastic head, near swords and walking sticks that sit cheek by jowl with movie posters and other bits and pieces of Greencastle's past. "It boggles my mind that on a daily basis I can come in here and just handle history," says Bonnie Shockey, the museum president, as she pulls down boxes filled with Civil War uniforms and other artifacts.

Emerson wasn't the only Greencastle resident who wished death to traitors. So did Tom Pawling. He owned the Antrim House, an inn that stood on the site of the current establishment of the same name on East Baltimore Street (although today's building dates from 1904). Pawling was so pro-Union that in the spring of 1861 he brought his own hanging rope to a hearing for some warehouse arsonists suspected of Southern sympathies. Fortunately for the firebugs, their motivation had been robbery, not secession.

Greencastle eventually had plenty of real secessionists to worry about. The first indications of their approach were the supply wagons of Milroy's command, which reached Greencastle on June 15, 1863, after their panicky flight down the Shenandoah Valley following the rout at Winchester. Like the animals who flee in advance of the hunters, the wagons served as a warning. Later that evening, the advancemen for the Confederate army reached Greencastle.

They belonged to a brigade of cavalry under the command of Brig. Gen. Albert Gallatin Jenkins. He had about 1,600 men and was serving under Brig. Gen. Robert E. Rodes, who commanded a division of Maj. Gen. Richard S. Ewell's II Corps.

Jenkins hailed from Virginia, but he had attended college in Pennsylvania and graduated from Harvard Law School. Jenkins had served in the U.S. Congress, and for a time he served in the Rebel Congress too, but left after receiving promotion to brigadier general. Soon after, he began taking a cavalry brigade on raids in Virginia and Ohio. He had short hair that retreated up his forehead, but the loss was more than compensated for by a great dark beard and mustache that spilled down his face and chest. The beard may have been similar to Jeb Stuart's, but Jenkins was a somewhat timid commander who lacked Stuart's flash and fire, although he did push further north into Pennsylvania than any other Confederate general.

Jenkins's stay in Greencastle was short, and he was soon on the road north to Chambersburg. Before long, rumors of Union soldiers sent him scurrying back again—just in time for his soldiers to ambush Corporal Rihl.

Jenkins had been just the beginning. The real flood of Confederate gray reached Greencastle on June 22, when Rodes and his brigade arrived, followed by the men of the I Corps under Lt. Gen. James Longstreet.

Private W. C. Ward of the 4th Alabama—which served in Brig. Gen. Evander Laws's brigade in Longstreet's corps—was in good spirits as he marched through Greencastle and heard the fifes and drums play "The Bonnie Blue Flag." "We were a merry lot," he remembered. "Entering the one long street of Greencastle, we found the people not at all afraid of us, as might have been expected." One of Ward's fellow soldiers snatched a new felt hat from the head of an older man and left his battered Confederate hat on the sidewalk in its place, one of many incidents of involuntary hat trading that occurred throughout Pennsylvania. "The old man seemed dazed," Ward said. "Rubbing his hands through his thin hair he . . . was overheard to say, 'I really believe that soldier has taken my hat.'" But the Rebels were after more than hats. In Greencastle, they demanded pistols, saddles, leather, lead, and food, typical of the demands they would make on towns throughout this portion of the state.

Dolly Harris lived with her family on North Carlisle Street. A bank building now occupies the site, but the rest of the street is lined with neat and well maintained homes that stood here when the long lines of Confederates streamed past. The story as recounted in W. P. Conrad and Ted Alexander's *War Passed This Way* is that as Maj. Gen. George Pickett's division passed up North Carlisle Street, Dolly Harris stood in front of her house with an American flag pinned to her apron and waved it defiantly at the Confederate general. "Traitors, traitors, come and take this flag, the man of you, who dares," she shouted. Instead of being offended, Pickett doffed his hat to the fervent Unionist and had his band strike up "Dixie."

The North celebrated Dolly Harris for her defiance, much as it had done for Barbara Fritchie when she allegedly flew the American flag in Fredericksburg, Maryland, during the Antietam campaign. Unlike Fritchie, Harris didn't have John Greenleaf Whittier to celebrate her in verse, although a number of lesser poets tried their hands. Wrote one:

She donned her apron, the "Flag of the Free,"
And stood on the sidewalk defiantly,
"Take this flag if you dare!" said she,
Flaunting the emblem of Liberty;
While twice ten thousand Southern men,
There marching by our heroine then.

A marker on the town's Diamond recalls another incident that took place in Greencastle, after the last Confederate had filed past the Harris house. On July 2, Union cavalrymen under Capt. Ulric Dahlgren rode into town. "If a band of angels had come down, they would not have been more unexpected. I may probably add, not so welcome," wrote one resident. "Their leader, the gallant Dahlgren, though a mere youth, had the entire confidence of his men and handled them with ease and skill." Command ran in the family, for Ulric Dahlgren was the son of Rear Admiral John Dahlgren, and had chosen the cavalry as his route to glory.

He found it, for a brief moment, in Greencastle. Enemy horsemen had been spotted heading toward town from the south, so Dahlgren set up an ambush in the Diamond and swiftly overwhelmed the Confederates. They turned out to be couriers with dispatches from Richmond for Robert E. Lee, informing the general that he could expect no help from the Confederate capital. Dahlgren delivered the papers to General Meade at Gettysburg, where they helped clarify the situation facing the Union army.

Dahlgren went on to die an inglorious death. On a mission led by Brig. Gen. Judson Kilpatrick in February 1864, he attempted to raid Richmond and free Union prisoners held there. Dahlgren was killed and papers on his body revealed plans to assassinate high-ranking Confederates, President Jefferson Davis among them. Union denials were unconvincing, and Southerners denounced Dahlgren as an unprincipled barbarian.

Mercersburg

Mercersburg is about ten miles west of Greencastle on Route 16. The route is largely rural, with a few townships along the way. Occasionally you can spy log cabin homes with their alternating bands of dark logs and white plaster, mute witnesses to centuries of travelers who passed this way. The landscape of rolling farmland, with the dark, brooding pres-

James Buchanan, Pennsylvania native and fifteenth President of the United States, was born in Mercersburg.
LIBRARY OF CONGRESS

ence of Tuscarora Mountain in the background, could almost be a vision from the 1860s.

Mercersburg's main street hasn't changed all that much since the 1860s, but the town has lost its international reputation. "Mercersburg was well known," says Tim Rockwell, a life-long resident, retired archeologist and former dean of students at Mercersburg Academy, a private boarding school. "In the nineteenth century, Mercersburg was often referred to as the Athens of south-central Pennsylvania." It had a world-renowned theological seminary, which stood on the site now occupied by the Mercersburg Academy. Marshall College called Mercersburg home until it moved to Lancaster to become part of Franklin and Marshall College. "It really was a place of literature and music," Rockwell says.

Like so many other towns, its central square was called the Diamond. The fountain that once stood in the center has been moved (it now sits on someone's lawn), but the street is still lined with handsome nineteenth-century buildings. A large brick building on the south side of the street below the Diamond is the former residence of Harriet Lane, the niece of Mercersburg's most famous resident, President James Buchanan. Across the street stands the James Buchanan Inn, a restaurant in the building where the future president lived from 1796 until 1829. Just up the street, opposite the main square, is a new three-quarter-scale statue of Buchanan.

Having James Buchanan as your native son is a mixed blessing. On the one hand, he was president of the United States. On the other, he wasn't a very good one, regularly landing near the bottom of any ranking of our chief executives. Buchanan also has to stand in the shadow of his successor, a man from Illinois named Abraham Lincoln. Still, he's a native son, and Mercersburg does what it can with him.

The log cabin where Buchanan was born now sits on the Mercersburg Academy grounds, in a grove of trees overlooking the outdoor track. Buchanan was born in 1791 in this little cabin with its steep, moss-covered roof and tall stone chimney. It looks like a child's drawing of a log cabin that has sprung to life.

The cabin led a nomadic existence after sheltering the infant future president. When Buchanan slid into the world in 1791, it stood west of Mercersburg in Cove Gap—now the site of the aptly named Buchanan Birthplace State Park. Like Buchanan himself, who moved into Mercersburg when he was six, the cabin was uprooted and taken into town. Years later, it was moved to Chambersburg, and then finally it arrived here in 1953.

Buchanan's Birthplace State Park is a peaceful setting in the woods that nestles against the beetling brow of Tuscarora Mountain. In Buchanan's time, this place was called Stony Batter, a name his father picked to salute his Irish homeland ("batter" in Gaelic means road). Even today, it feels like the frontier, nestled among tall pines on Buck's Run below the mountain's steep, forested slope. Buchanan Sr. established a trading post here and did a good business supplying settlements to the west over the mountain. It's easy to imagine teamsters coaching their reluctant pack animals up the trail—traces of which remain—on their way to their customers. Young James remembered his birthplace as "a rugged but romantic spot" where he found "the mountains and

The log cabin that was James Buchanan's birthplace is on the campus of Mercersburg Academy.

Mercersburg

Visit **Mercersburg Academy**, 300 E. Seminary St., to see the James Buchanan cabin, but make a point to visit the school's chapel. Dedicated in 1928, the Gothic structure contains some beautiful stained-glass windows. (717) 328-6314, www.mercersburg.edu.

The **Zion Union Cemetery**, Bennett Ave., includes the graves of thirty-six black veterans of the Civil War, including members of the 54th Massachusetts. From Route 16, turn onto Linden Ave., then right on Fairview Ave., then left onto Bennett, which dead-ends at the cemetery.

mountain stream under the scenery captivating." James was six when the Buchanan family moved to Mercersburg. Eventually the cabin followed, like a pet that had been left behind by accident.

In the cabin's place stands a somewhat odd memorial to Buchanan, a thirty-one-foot-tall stone pyramid behind an iron fence and beneath improbably tall, straight pines. This weighty tribute, all 300 tons of it, is the legacy of niece Harriet Lane, who left $100,000 in her will for monuments to her uncle's legacy. Still, it's done little for the reputation of the man one crony called "the incorruptible statesman whose work was upon the mountain ranges of the law."

Incorruptible he may have been, but Buchanan could not stop the country from sliding into Civil War. That war reached Mercersburg on October 10, 1862, when Jeb Stuart came calling.

Stuart and his 1,800 handpicked men reached Mercersburg on a nasty, rainy morning. While his chief of artillery, the youthful Captain John Pelham, set up two of the raiders' four cannon on Mercersburg's Diamond, Stuart rested at Bridgeside, a stone house down Main Street on the banks of Smith's Run. It belonged to the Steigers family then, and still does now, serving as the law office of Steigers, Steigers, and Myers. When Stuart appeared out of the rain, George Steigers was away selling livestock. Mrs. Steigers informed her uninvited guest that her children were sick with German measles, so Stuart wisely remained outside, and asked Mrs. Steigers to serve him a late breakfast on the side porch.

In the meantime, Stuart's men captured several prominent citizens, whom they planned to exchange for Confederates in Union prisons. After the raiders left Mercersburg on their way toward Chambersburg, they also bagged George Steigers, who was heading back to the home the Confederates had just left. Steigers managed to slip away from his captors in a cornfield, but the Confederates kept his coach and horses. His descendents still have the note of reimbursement for $286.40 the Federal government issued after the war.

From his beautiful house on Main Street—built in 1888 on the site of a hotel that stood here during the Civil War—John W. Thompson IV can gaze across the creek and see Bridgeside. Thompson is the local expert on Stuart's raid, having published two books on the topic. He even had an ancestor—Daniel A. Grimsley of the 6th Virginia Calvary—who rode with Stuart and may have been here in 1862. Thompson started researching the raid for a talk he gave to the Mercersburg Historical Society, but the project took on a life of its own. "The thing that was most untapped was this area, Franklin County," he says. "The reason it probably hadn't been done before was everybody was pro-Northern. Who wants to write about a Southern raid that embarrassed the North? So I realized there was a lot to be uncovered."

In 2002 Thompson even helped organize a 140th anniversary reenactment of the raid. He held a reception at his home, with guests dressed as Confederate officers—Thompson had his own uniform specially made—and there was a ball at the Mercersburg Academy. Thompson also commissioned three paintings by artist Ron Lesser. One of them, showing Stuart and some of his men on Mercersburg's Diamond, hangs in the Academy library.

Stuart's men were just the beginning of Mercersburg's Confederate troubles. Various groups of Rebel horsemen reached town in the weeks leading up to Gettysburg in 1863. Members of John Singleton Mosby's cavalry passed through and took horses on June 19, and more raiders arrived later that month. The least savory aspect of some of these raids was the capture of African Americans—some of them born free—whom the Confederates brought back south to slavery. Mercersburg had a large free black population, and when word spread that the Confederates were on their way, many African Americans fled north. Some who didn't soon regretted the decision. Dr. Philip Schaff, who taught at the Mercersburg Theological Seminary, recorded in his diary watching

Confederates round up African Americans. He said it was "the worst spectacle I ever saw in this war."

Brig. Gen. John Imboden and his cavalry reached town on June 30 and the general demanded supplies for his men. "When Imboden came in, it was one of the roughest times," says Tim Rockwell. Imboden divided the town into quadrants so his men could systematically round up goods from the residents. Then a messenger arrived from Greencastle on a mule, and Imboden and his men moved out of town immediately, leaving all the confiscated goods piled up in the streets. "The reason for their haste was that they received orders to get to Chambersburg to relieve Pickett, so Pickett could move forward."

While battle raged at Gettysburg on July 3, Mercersburg had a little excitement of its own. Two Union soldiers, perhaps stragglers from Milroy's division, were at the Mansion House, the large stone hotel that still stands on the square, when they received word that three Confederate cavalrymen were headed into town. They were scouts from the 12th Virginia Cavalry, and when they rode into the Diamond, the two Federals opened fire from alongside the Mansion House, wounding Lt. William Cane and killing Private J. W. Alban. The third Confederate escaped. "Those who saw the affair say that after the shot was fired, Alban never moved, and no one knew that he had been shot until his horse walked slowly over to the corner at Fallon's hardware store," read a contemporary account. "When the horse stopped at a tree box, the rider fell off, and for the first time was it known that he had been shot." The two Union soldiers then disappeared from town.

Citizens buried the dead man in a brick kiln, but dug him up and reburied him in the old Presbyterian cemetery, then moved him again to the more bucolic setting of Evergreen Cemetery just outside of town, opposite the Mercersburg Inn. Also there in company with Alban is a pair of Confederate soldiers who were wounded at Gettysburg and died in Mercersburg. They were two of the many Confederate wounded who were treated in hastily organized hospitals in the town's churches and seminary buildings after Union cavalrymen captured their wagon train.

Mercersburg had another brief encounter with the Confederacy on July 29, 1864, when Brig. Gen. John McCausland came riding through. In Mercersburg, about thirty men of the 6th U.S. Cavalry fought a valiant delaying action through town. The Union horsemen would fire a volley, ride off, set up another ambush for another volley, then ride off again.

The grave of Confederate private J. W. Alban, a scout shot in Mercersburg, stands aside the stones of two Confederate casualties of Gettysburg in the Evergreen Cemetery.

At one point, the Federals set up their ambush right in Mercersburg's Diamond. "They reach the Diamond," a resident wrote. "Our few men receive them with a fire and retreat coolly down the street, the rebels after them and bullets flying. One struck near our house." The Confederates finally drove their nettlesome attackers off, then rested for a time before saddling up again and heading off toward Chambersburg.

Chambersburg

"No town in the Northern States is more inseparably interwoven with the thrilling events of the late war, than Chambersburg," wrote Alexander K. McClure in 1883. He may have been a little biased. McClure was a lawyer, political leader, and the editor and publisher of the Chambersburg *Repository and Transcript*. He lived in Chambersburg during the war, and Confederate officers sometimes relied on the coerced hospitality of his house outside town.

Brig. Gen. John McCausland's soldiers burned that house to the ground in 1864 when they torched Chambersburg. McClure rebuilt it, and now Wilson College uses the huge, white-brick Victorian building as its admissions office, Norland Hall. Portraits of McClure and his wife grace the front hallway beneath lofty, eighteen-foot ceilings. Upstairs in another office, a glass case holds some McClure mementos, including a press badge to the 1900 Republican convention and a small watercolor portrait.

Personal bias aside, McClure had a point. Chambersburg attracted war like a magnet.

The best starting point for exploring the city's Civil War history is at the Chambersburg Heritage Center, right in the middle of town on the main square, which, as in Mercersburg and Greencastle, is called the Diamond. The Diamond is guarded by the bronze statue of a Civil War soldier, who faces south down Main Street as though to ward off invaders, although flesh-and-blood soldiers didn't do much warding off during the war.

The Heritage Center occupies the former Valley National Bank building, and even has some exhibits inside the old bank vault, its huge round door now open permanently. Other exhibits in the main room tell Chambersburg's story, from the building of a fort here by Benjamin Chambers in 1756, through twentieth-century transportation history. A small glass case holds some relics from the fires of 1864— a chunk of burned timber from a house that felt the Confederates' wrath, and a pewter coffeepot that was warped by the heat.

Unfortunately for seekers of Civil War history, the fire obliterated much of it. There are a few survivors. The columns on the county courthouse were salvaged from the courthouse that burned in 1864, and the Masonic Temple on the corner of Second and Queen streets survived the attack. According to legend, Confederate Masons stood guard to make sure no one burned it.

Another prewar survivor stands on King Street, and some Chambersburg residents thought this little house might explain the Confederates' wrath.

A bronze Union soldier stands on Chambersburg's Diamond facing south in symbolic defense against rebel marauders.

Confederate Masons ensured the survival of the Masonic Temple in Chambersburg while the rest of the town burned.

For a brief time, the white clapboard building with weathered black shutters, now an office for the American Heart Association, provided a home for John Brown.

Brown pulled into town, under the name of Isaac Smith, in 1859, and rented rooms from Mary Ritner here as he made plans for his raid on Harpers Ferry. Brown's plan was to raid the town, capture the Federal arsenal there, and use the arms, plus pikes he had ordered, to start a slave rebellion.

Brown met Frederick Douglass at a quarry outside of Chambersburg, and there sought to enlist the noted abolitionist—himself an escaped slave—into his plans. The quarry is gone, but a historical marker indicates the spot, behind a shopping center, up against trees that line a little creek. "I approached the old quarry very cautiously, for John Brown was generally well armed, and regarded strangers with suspicion," Douglass reported. He found Brown pretending to be fishing. "The taking of Harpers Ferry, of which Captain Brown had merely hinted at before, was now declared as his settled purpose, and he wanted to know what I thought of it. I at once opposed the measure with all the arguments at my command." Douglass could not deter Brown, and the raid he launched that October helped widen the sectional divisions that led to Civil War.

Another survivor from 1864 is a big brick building with the white cupola on the corner of Second and King streets. It's the old Franklin County Jail, which dates from 1818. The rebels would have been pleased to know that one of John Brown's raiders had been imprisoned here after Harpers Ferry. Alexander McClure hoped to concoct a plan to help him escape, but didn't have time. Today the building is the headquarters for the Kittochtinny Historical Society.

Once the war that Brown helped start finally erupted, McClure plunged into the thick of things. He served as an assistant adjutant general for Governor Curtin, helped recruit troops, and headed a small intelligence operation that gathered information about Confederate movements and forwarded it to Harrisburg. When Stuart's raiders came galloping into town in 1862 after their visit to Mercersburg, McClure was on their list of people to capture. McClure was walking across the Diamond when a man slapped him on the back. He turned to see Hugh Logan, a former client who had enlisted in the Confederate army and was serving as a scout for Stuart. Fortunately for McClure, Logan was "one of the rugged mountaineers in whom you will often find the most devoted personal friendship," McClure wrote. "'Jeb' wants you d——d badly," Logan warned him.

McClure walked back to his house, where he found the Confederates had already taken ten of his horses. Settling himself on his front porch,

 ## Chambersburg

The **Chambersburg Heritage Center**, 100 Lincoln Way East on Memorial Square, is housed in a former bank building that dates from 1915. Its exhibits cover the entire history of Chambersburg, including the Civil War years. This is also the place to purchase brochures ($1.00 each) for five driving tours that cover various aspects of the area's history, including two Civil War tours, "Invasions and Raids" and "The Freedom Trail." The center is open Monday through Friday from 8 AM to 5 PM, Saturday from 10 AM until 3 PM, and Sunday (Memorial Day until Labor Day) from noon until 3 PM (717) 264-7101, www.chambersburg.org. Each year the Greater Chambersburg Chamber of Commerce sponsors the **Chambersburg Civil War Seminars**. Coordinated by Ted Alexander, the chief historian at Antietam and an authority on local Civil War history, the seminars attract distinguished participants each year. Contact the chamber for more information.

Cedar Grove Cemetery, Franklin St., contains many Union veterans. The cemetery was established in 1854, and when the Confederates burned the town ten years later, many residents went here to escape the flames. Dolly Harris of Greencastle, who married John Lesher and moved to Chambersburg, is buried here. **Lebanon Cemetery**, off U.S. Route 30 west of town, was the town's African American burial ground. It slopes down from the top of a hill that offers great views across Chambersburg. Many members of the United States Colored Troops are buried here, as are Henry Watson and Joseph R. Winters, two men involved with John Brown and the Underground Railroad.

he waited. Around midnight, a squad of Confederate cavalry appeared out of the darkness. McClure served them dinner and discussed the war with them afterwards. The men talked into the night until the sound of "Boots and Saddles" announced the dawn. The Confederates shook hands with their host, thanked him for his hospitality, mounted their horses and rode off. "I thus had a most interesting and impressive night with the Confederates, whose sense of chivalry made them refuse to obey the order to arrest me because they had entered my home in quest of hospitality," McClure wrote.

Ten years passed before McClure learned the identity of his guests. On a trip to Washington he met Thomas W. Whitehead, a congressman from Virginia, who said he had been one of the soldiers.

Rebels returned to Chambersburg in 1863. On the night of June 15, Jacob Hoke, who had a home and store on the Diamond, was seated at a window when he heard horses approaching. The street was dark, with only gas lamps in front of a bank offering any light. The horsemen turned out to belong to Jenkins' cavalry. Two hundred more men soon followed, and then Jenkins himself, who made himself comfortable at McClure's home. This time, McClure was "prudently absent."

In the morning, the Confederates "purchased" material from local stores with Confederate money. They also started capturing blacks, who fled into surrounding wheatfields only to be chased down by mounted cavalrymen. Then rumors of approaching Union forces persuaded the jittery Jenkins to remove himself back to Greencastle. The timidity so peeved General Ewell that he complained to Lee, but Lee merely counseled him to assign a staff officer to keep an eye on the skittish cavalry commander.

It was only a temporary reprieve. On the morning of June 24, Rodes's division reached Chambersburg, riding into town to the tune of "The Bonnie Blue Flag." One-legged General Ewell arrived in a carriage. Hoke described him as "a thin, sallow-faced man, with strongly-marked Southern features, and a head and physiognomy which strongly indicated culture, refinement and genius." He set up his headquarters in the Franklin Hotel. Generals Lee and A. P. Hill soon followed.

Hoke watched Robert E. Lee consult with Hill in the Diamond. "General Lee, as he sat on his horse that day in the public square of Chambersburg, looked every inch a soldier," Hoke wrote. "He was at that time about fifty-two years of age, stoutly built, of medium height, hair strongly mixed with gray, and a rough gray beard. He wore the usual Confederate gray, with some little ornamentation about the collar of his coat. His hat was a soft black without ornament other than a military cord around the crown. His whole appearance indicated dignity, composure, and disregard for the gaudy trappings of war and the honor attaching to his high station."

Lee set up his headquarters in a place then called Shetter's, and later Messersmith's, Woods. There's a marker near the spot on U.S. Route 30 in front of a Pizza Hut. There's nothing woodsy about the scene now, although some pastoralism survives in the cemetery behind the restaurant. Lee might have winced at its name—Lincoln Cemetery.

Lee was at Chambersburg when he ordered his army to converge at Gettysburg. A spy named Harrison had reached Longstreet's headquarters and told the general that the Union army was already over the Potomac and on the move north. Longstreet sent Harrison over to Lee at Messersmith's Woods. Soon afterward, the long columns of Confederate soldiers were marching eastward toward the battle that would end Lee's Pennsylvania campaign.

Even worse was yet to come for Chambersburg, and it arrived in 1864. Maj. Gen. John McCausland was of Irish descent, but his cropped hair and mustache with drooping waxed tips gave him a Teutonic look. McCausland had taken over Albert Jenkins's cavalry following Jenkins's death in West Virginia. He served under Jubal Early, who was outraged by Maj. Gen. David Hunter's destruction of Confederate property in the Shenandoah Valley. "I came to the conclusion it was time to open the

Chambersburg was in ruins after McCausland's forces plundered and burned the town in 1864. PENNSYLVANIA STATE ARCHIVES (MG-218)

eyes of the North to this enormity, by an example in the way of retaliation," Early wrote.

McCausland's brigade, augmented by cavalry under Brig. Gen. Bradley T. Johnson, passed through Mercersburg on July 29 and headed to Chambersburg. Outside of town, on the hills to the west, McCausland set up his headquarters in the Greenawalt House. The house is there today, a rambling white building with a side porch ornamented by gingerbread trim. Here, early on the morning of July 30, McCausland met with his officers and, in a rancorous session, told them he planned to burn the town if Chambersburg couldn't come up with a cash ransom.

McCausland set up his artillery on this hill and had three shots fired into Chambersburg. He then sent his chief of staff to the courthouse to present his demands. The town was neither willing nor able to comply, so McCausland's men set to work. They removed furniture from homes, piled it in heaps, and set it on fire. They set fires in closets and bureaus. Some of them took to the work with "evident delight," reported Jacob Hoke. "Others, to their credit be it said, entirely disapproved of the work, and only entered upon it because compelled to do so." William E. Peters, who commanded the 21st Virginia Cavalry, refused to participate. As a result, he was placed under arrest.

Soon the center of town was in flames. "The conflagration at its height was a scene of surpassing grandeur and terror," wrote Hoke, who reported seeing a fire-fueled column—"A whirling, hissing, and sucking cone"—hurl clothing, pillows, quilts, and on one occasion, a four-year-old girl into the air.

The events in Chambersburg so moved resident Samuel L. Fisher that he wrote a copiously footnoted poem called "The Burning of Chambersburg" and published it in 1879. Part of it reads:

> At last the torch they yet applied
> To well arranged combustibles;
> And from the place away they hied,
> Lest they to harm expose themselves.
>
> Then followed scenes none can describe,
> So terrible are all and each;
> You may imagination bribe,
> But yet must fail the truth to reach.

The flames in all directions rised;
Devour whate'er may intervene;
With brightness they light up the skies,
Attracting birds to the strange scene.

In a footnote, Fisher explained, "The whole sky was lit up with a fearful glare, and high in the air, multitudes of birds of various kinds were moving strangely around in wide majestic circles over the burning town." Brig. Gen. William Averell, the Union cavalry commander who should have defended Chambersburg, was instead down in Greencastle. Darius Couch, commander of the department of the Susquehanna, sent telegrams ordering Averell to intercept McCausland, but Averell's men couldn't find their commander. He later said he had fallen asleep against a fence at the Fleming farm, the same spot where Corporal Rihl had died the year before. Chambersburg was a smoking ruin by the time Averell reached it. He finally caught up with the Confederates outside McConnellsburg, drove them from Union soil, and eventually routed them in West Virginia.

That was too late to help the people of Chambersburg. Fortunately, no one was killed during the attack, though one man died later, possibly of smoke inhalation. Damage was considerable. Almost 300 buildings had been lost, not counting smaller sheds, outbuildings, and thirty-eight stables and barns. Also lost were sixty-nine pianos. Before burning one of them, a Rebel had danced up and down the keyboard, "remarking that it was in that way they made music in Virginia." Three thousand people were left homeless, and the state later calculated the damage at $1,628,431.

Jubal Early, who had ordered the burning, felt no remorse. "For this act I, alone, am responsible, as the officers engaged in it were simply executing my orders, and had no discretion left them," he wrote after the war. "Notwithstanding the lapse of time which has occurred and the result of the war, I see no reason to regret my conduct on this occasion." Neither, apparently, did McCausland. Instead of surrendering with Robert E. Lee at Appomattox, he left the country, not returning until 1867. For the rest of his life, he lived in relative seclusion on a farm in West Virginia. He died in 1927 at the age of ninety.

Other Nearby Points of Interest

Off Route 30, about halfway between Chambersburg and Gettysburg, is the site of the Caledonia Iron Furnace once owned by Congressman Thaddeus Stevens. A 1927 reproduction of his blacksmith shop stands at the edge of a field by the highway, and at the parking lot on the other side of Route 233 you can find a reproduction of Stevens's huge iron furnace. Unfortunately for Stevens, Jubal Early found the works on June 26 as he marched toward Gettysburg. "I determined to destroy them," he recalled. Early knew that Stevens, a radical Republican and an ardent abolitionist, was no friend of the South, so in defiance of Lee's orders not to destroy civilian property, he had the iron works burned. Today, the site of Stevens's works is part of Caledonia State Park, which offers camping, swimming, picnicking—and hiking along the Thaddeus Stevens Historic Trail.

From Mercersburg heading west, Route 16 makes a dizzying rise and fall up and down Tuscarora Mountain and into the Fulton County borough of McConnellsburg. This little town saw its share of Civil War raids. Just outside of town on Route 16, as the road finishes its steep descent down the western face of Tuscarora Mountain, there's a monument to a pair of Confederate soldiers who were killed here on June 29, 1863. The concrete memorial erected by the United Daughters of the Confederacy claims it was the first battle on Pennsylvania soil. Corp. William Rihl, who was killed in Greencastle a week earlier, might disagree.

VISITING Other Nearby Points of Interest

For information on **Caledonia State Park**, call 717-352-2161. McConnellsburg is in neighboring Fulton County. Contact the **Fulton County Chamber of Commerce** at 717-485-4064. **The Waynesboro Area Industrial Heritage Trust** is located at 235 Philadelphia Ave. and is open by appointment, 717-762-4460. **The Renfew Museum and Park** at 1010 E. Main St. is open April 22 through October on Tuesday through Sunday from noon to 4 PM (last tour at 3:30 PM). There is an admission charge. Grounds are open free of charge from dawn to dusk. (717) 762-4723, www.renfrewmuseum.org.

A marker for "The Last Confederate Bivouac North of the Mason-Dixon Line," south of town on Route 522, commemorates the end of McConnellsburg's war, when Union troops under Brig. Gen. William A. Averell drove the last Confederates from Northern soil. The bivouacers in question were led by Brig. Gen. Bradley T. Johnson, fresh from the burning of Chambersburg.

Continue east on Route 16 from Greencastle and you'll reach the town of Waynesboro. Jubal Early made his way into Pennsylvania through this town, and portions of Lee's army—including Lee himself—made their way out along the same route. The Waynesboro Area Industrial Heritage Trust showcases the region's industrial history and is housed in a former church. The Renfew Museum and Park has 107 acres of woods and farmland centered around a restored farmstead, just the kind of place the invading Confederates would visit to gather food and supplies.

Cumberland County
Up the Valley

Shippensburg

Shippensburg has a typical Pennsylvania main street—straight and wide and lined by low-porched houses and small businesses. The town doesn't have its classic Diamond anymore, but it used to be at the intersection of King and Earl streets, with the Select Family Restaurant standing where the Union Hotel once overlooked the square in 1863. Poised between two county seats, Chambersburg to the south and Carlisle to the north, Civil War Shippensburg had a population of around 1,800 people. The main street was known as the Harrisburg Pike, the macadamized toll road that led up the Cumberland Valley to the state capital.

In June 1863, rumors of war stirred Shippensburg, and then wagons from Milroy's Winchester command came clattering down the pike, escorted by Capt. William Boyd and Company C of the 1st New York Cavalry. On June 19, about 800 men of the 8th and 71st New York National Guard under Brig. Gen. Joseph Knipe reached town by rail from Harrisburg. The Pennsylvania Battery of Militia under Captain E. Spenser arrived too, with four guns and 300 more men. The storm clouds were gathering.

On Wednesday, June 24, word reached Shippensburg that the Rebels were approaching. The owner of the Union Hotel hastily painted over his sign, afraid it would goad the Confederates. Other residents climbed on roofs to get a better view—and to get out of the line of fire, if that proved necessary. "To say that all Shippensburg stood on its head is to describe the excitement existing there that Wednesday morning in immoderately modest terms," a resident wrote in an account published in the Harrisburg *Sunday Telegram.* Boyd and his men had returned from Harrisburg and pushed on down to Greencastle, but at around two o'clock they came galloping through town from the south, mounted Confederates in hot pursuit. General Jenkins arrived about an hour later. "In figure Jenkins was as straight as an arrow," an eyewitness noted. "Above medium height with a sandy beard, fully a foot long, and eyes that could look stern or twinkle with good-humor merriement [*sic*] as occasion required. The Shippensburgers agreed that the general looked like a good fellow and a gentleman." Jenkins set up a headquarters and demanded food for his men.

One of the residents who met with the general was probably William McLean, whose red-brick house still stands at 49 West King Street. McLean operated a tannery on Branch Creek behind his home. McLean knew the Confederates were desperate for leather, so he asked his employees to hide as much as they could beneath false bottoms in the soaking vats, and the rest beneath a pile of hastily stacked wood. Thomas Blair, who sold grain and produce, was not so sly. The Confederates took $30,000 of his stock, which was earmarked for the Federal government. John McPherson, who had a hardware store on King Street, lost some of his inventory to the Confederates too, but before they arrived, he hid his more valuable items in his fireplaces, and then wallpapered them over. A hardware store still does business in McPherson's building at 35 West King Street. It is the oldest business in Shippensburg, and perhaps the oldest hardware store in Pennsylvania.

George McLean saved his leather, but he and his wife, Nancy, suffered a worse loss during the war. Their son, George Jr., had been mortally wounded during the battle of Fredericksburg the previous December. His parents visited him in a Washington, D.C., hospital before he died, two days before Christmas in 1862. For the McLeans, the arrival of enemy soldiers literally on their very doorstep must have aroused strong emotions. Yet one night Nancy McLean heard violent coughing from one of the young Confederates camped on her front porch. She felt sorry for him, so in the morning she and her daughter made coffee and fresh bread with apple butter for the soldiers. The Southerners had never seen apple butter before and, afraid it might be

Confederate soldiers camped at Dykeman's Spring, formerly Indian Springs, during their brief stop in Shippensburg.

poison, began scraping it off their bread. The McLeans reassured them it was safe.

Two days after Jenkins reached Shippensburg, the Confederate infantry began streaming into town. First to arrive was a brigade under Brig. Gen. Junius Daniel, part of Robert Rodes's division. Some of the soldiers set up camp at a spot just outside of town called Indian Springs, known now as Dykeman's Spring. Today it's a small park with a trail that winds over wooden bridges and through wetlands. On top of a hill looking over a pond stands a Victorian building, the Dykeman House bed and breakfast. George Dykeman built this striking Italiante mansion around the original brick farmhouse in 1870.

The Confederates didn't tarry long in Shippensburg. They began moving out on June 27 on their way to Carlisle and eventually, they hoped, Harrisburg. It must have been a sight to see, when a single division, under Edward Johnson, had a wagon train that stretched for fourteen miles.

Even as Robert E. Lee had planned the invasion that brought these troops to Shippensburg, some Shippensburg residents were preparing to fight for the Union—but they had to leave Pennsylvania to get the opportunity. The Shirk brothers—John, James, and Casper—were black. Pennsylvania didn't start enlisting African Americans until June 1863, and by then the Shirks had already joined Massachusetts black regiments, including the 54th Massachusetts.

The Shirks are among the twenty-six or so African American soldiers from the Civil War buried in Locust Grove Cemetery on North Queen Street. The cemetery is narrow, bounded on each side by a couple of tawdry looking houses. (One of them is the former American Legion post for African Americans.) All the stones are weathered except for a new one that marks the grave of Joseph Lane, who served in Company G of the 22nd Regiment of the U.S. Colored Volunteer Infantry. Lane received a new stone in 2005 after a man who maintained a cemetery in Huntingdon County read that Locust Grove had been vandalized. "So often you read bad news in the paper and there's nothing you can do about it," Matthew Whitsel told the *Shippensburg Sentinel.* "I just thought that maybe there was something I could do in this case." Whitsel contacted the department of veterans affairs, which supplied the new gravestone.

Locust Grove Cemetery in Shippensburg, the resting place of more than two dozen African American soldiers.

Lane's bright white marker is a sign that things might be looking up for the long-neglected cemetery. In 1949 local historian William Burkhart stumbled across the cemetery when he was placing flags on veterans' graves for Memorial Day. He found the place covered with weeds and littered with trash and broken bottles. Half the headstones were broken or toppled over. His curiosity piqued, Burkhart began researching the men who were buried here. He visited elderly members of the black community to tap their memories, and he canvassed service records.

Burkhart discovered a little bit about the three Shirk brothers. They were working in the local charcoal industry when they enlisted. John joined the 54th Massachusetts, the pioneering black regiment profiled in the 1989 movie *Glory*, and suffered a back injury during the campaign to capture Battery Wagner near Charleston, South Carolina. Casper's history is uncertain. He apparently joined Company E of the 5th Massachusetts Cavalry and died in Texas on October 31, 1865, and is buried in Louisiana. James joined the 55th Massachusetts.

Burkhart's research helped give the Shirks and the other forgotten soldiers here a second life. He found that Robert Green, a sergeant from Company E of the 127th Regiment, "became demented over religious matters" and was institutionalized before his death in 1894 at the age of fifty-nine. Samuel Cotton of Company L, 2nd Regiment of the U.S. Cavalry Colored Volunteers, was "a short, tough muscled little man with a very keen sense of humor." He died in 1901 at the age of fifty-five. Joseph Lane, the man with the new stone, "lived a rather unrestrained life after his return from the war," Burkhart noted. At one point he was unjustly accused of murder and jailed in Chambersburg until he was acquitted—an experience that turned him toward religion.

Dr. Steven Burg, a professor at Shippensburg University, and his students have added to Burkhart's work and hope to save Locust Grove from the ravages of time and neglect. "The first priority is to get a new fence around the cemetery," Burg says. "There's also some interest in doing some conservation work on the tombstones that are existing, identifying the sites particularly of the veterans who don't have tombstones and ordering those through veterans affairs." He'd like to add a flagpole and maybe a rostrum for Veterans Day or Memorial Day observances.

Burg says there are between twenty-six and twenty-eight black veterans buried here. With a black population of about 170 people in 1870, that

Shippensburg

Each year in June, Shippensburg holds the **March to Destiny Civil War Living History Encampment**, which offers period music and dancing, artillery and living history demonstrations, and other entertainments.

The **Shippensburg Historical Society**, 52 W. King St., was founded in 1945 and is housed in a building from the late eighteenth century. In a back room, cabinets along the walls hold 1,277 glass goblets that a local man spent forty years collecting. Upstairs, a room has models and dioramas constructed locally for the Works Progress Administration during the Depression. There are a few Civil War relics too. The museum is open for tours Wednesday and Saturday, 1 PM to 4 PM, or by appointment. (717) 532-6727. The Historical Society is also the co-sponsor of the **Locust Grove Cemetery Restoration Campaign**, a movement to raise funds for the cemetery on N. Queen St. For more information, call (717) 532-7307 or (717) 532-5642.

Several of Shippensburg's buildings have Civil War connections. The house at **20 West King Street** was the boyhood home of Brig. Gen. Samuel Sturgis. Before the Battle of Second Bull Run, Sturgis was heard to comment about Maj. Gen. John Pope, "I don't care for John Pope one pinch of owl dung!" His division was later soundly defeated by Confederate Maj. Gen. Nathan Bedford Forrest at the Battle of Brice's Cross Roads in April 1864. Sturgis died in Minnesota in 1889.

The white brick building with columned porch at **110 East King Street** was the home of James Kelso, who raised men from Shippensburg to form Company D of the 130th Pennsylvania Volunteers. When the Rebels learned that the house was the home of a Union officer, they looted it.

The little yellow house at **340 East King Street** was the home of Regina Agle, who became known as the "Widow Agle" after her husband, Jacob, was killed in action in Georgia on September 13, 1863. Regina raised their three sons by herself and never remarried. She died in 1898.

The Agles, the Kelsos, the McCleans, and many others with stories from the Civil War are buried in **Spring Hill Cemetery**. The cemetery entrance is off North Morris Street.

was a significant chunk of the population, he notes. "Some of the people buried here simply wanted to get involved following Lee's invasion and the creation of the Massachusetts regiments," he says. Only about eight of the veterans buried here were born in Shippensburg. Emancipated and runaway slaves began reaching the area before the war, and they began joining the army once they got the opportunity in 1863.

By the time the war ended, 200,000 African Americans had served in the Union military. "When victory is won," said President Lincoln, who had initially been reluctant to enlist black troops, "there will be some black men who can remember that, with silent tongue and clenched teeth, and steady eye and well-poised bayonet, they have helped mankind to this great consummation."

Carlisle

On one of the Carlisle Courthouse's weathered sandstone columns, someone has painted "July 1863" in a prominent pock mark. A brick below a gash in a first-floor window ledge is dated similarly.

In Carlisle, such holes and nicks are called "Lee's Calling Cards" and people marked them so they wouldn't get accidentally "repaired." The Lee in question is not Gen. Robert E. Lee, but his nephew, Brig. Gen. Fitzhugh Lee, who commanded a brigade of cavalry under Jeb Stuart. The younger Lee was an accomplished cavalryman in his own right, and a respected subordinate to Stuart, with whom he shared a preference for a big, spade-shaped beard. Lee was also quite familiar with Carlisle, having served as a cavalry instructor at the Carlisle Barracks before the war. His friends knew him as "Fitz." After July 1, 1863, Carlisle called him "this monster Lee."

Carlisle had a rich history before the Civil War. The town was founded in 1751, when this region was still considered the frontier, and it became a major center for transportation into the western hinterlands. Benjamin Franklin, George Washington, and Major John André—Benedict Arnold's British contact for the plot to betray West Point, later hanged as a spy—all passed through town at some point.

Carlisle can also boast of a long military history. Carlisle Barracks, established in 1757, is the country's second oldest army post. Today it houses the Army's War College and it is open to the public, albeit only after visitors pass through fairly rigorous security. Once on post, the overall feeling is less of a military installation than a large college cam-

Shell damage on a column of the Cumberland County Courthouse preserves the essence of war in Carlisle.

Recreated Civil War cabins help bring the past to life at the Army Heritage and Education Center in Carlisle.

pus. The oldest building is the Hessian Powder Magazine, a small limestone building built in 1777, supposedly with the forced labor of Hessian prisoners captured at the Battle of Trenton. Not far away, beyond the big-porched commandant's quarters—burned by the Confederates in 1863 and since rebuilt—a little grove called Dragoon Circle commemorates the cavalry school that opened here in 1838. Fitzhugh Lee, of course, knew it well.

Like the prodigal son, Lee found his way back to Carlisle, a town that was bracing for war in June 1863. "The information that the rebels were upon us, seriously affected the nerves of some of our citizens," the *Carlisle American* reported in its July 15 edition. "The females, of course, were much alarmed and a scene of confusion and excitement ensued, which we will not attempt to describe."

It's safe to assume that the men of Jenkins's cavalry alarmed more than just the females when they rode slowly into town at about eleven o'clock on Saturday, June 27. "They were about four hundred in number, mounted infantry, and every man carried his gun in a position to use it on the instant, with his hand on the hammer," the paper reported. Jenkins met with prominent citizens in the town square and demanded rations. The citizens complied, and soon the stalls in the town market shed—now gone—were filling with food.

Ewell's infantry came marching down Pitt Street at five o'clock that afternoon to the sound of "Dixie" being played at the head of the column. "The men of the command presented a sorry appearance," reported the *Carlisle American.* "Many were barefooted, others hatless, numbers of them ragged, and all dirty." Ewell made his way to the barracks and established headquarters there. It was a homecoming of sorts for Old Bald Head, too, as he had studied there before the war and still had many social connections in town.

The men of Rodes's division bivouacked on the grounds of Dickinson College, in front of the gray limestone building of the West College—familiarly known merely as Old West. It has changed little since then. Engraved over the sweeping, arched doorway of the building is an inscription reading: "Dickinson College. Founded A.D. 1783. Burned down 1803. Rebuilt 1804." It seems a little more detail, perhaps, than a mere inscription warrants, but it's accurate. After the original brick building burned to the ground, Benjamin Latrobe, the architect of the U.S. Capitol in Washington, volunteered to design a new building for free. He had it built of limestone instead of the original brick, and Latrobe's building has proven fire resistant so far.

"Old West" on the Dickinson College campus served as a backdrop to an encampment of Maj. Gen. Robert Rodes's division.

Carlisle

The current **Courthouse**, Hanover and Church Sts., was built in 1846 to replace a 1766 structure that burned. In 1847 it was the site of the McLintock Riot, a "frightful melee" that erupted over attempts to prevent fugitive slaves from being returned to bondage in Maryland. Dr. John McLintock was a Dickinson College professor who intervened on behalf of the fugitives. Next to the courthouse is the **Veterans' Square**, which includes a monument to the men from Cumberland County who died in the Civil War.

Researchers interested in army history will want to visit the **U. S. Army Heritage and Education Center**, 950 Soldiers Dr. The Center, still growing, will eventually include the Army Military History Institute, the Army Heritage Museum, and a Visitors and Education Center. Outside, the mile-long Army Heritage Trail winds through a field alongside I-81 and includes exhibits and hardware. Inside, the collections include in the neighborhood of 90,000 images, plus letters, journals, and other documents. The collections are housed in the Ridgeway Hall, which opened in 2004. It's open weekdays from 9 AM to 4:45 PM. There is no charge for admission. (717) 245-3971, www.carlisle.army.mil/ahec.

The **Cumberland County Historical Society**, 21 N. Pitt St., includes a fine research area, and a museum on the second floor with Civil War relics, including a cannonball that went through the roof of 127 N. Hanover St., and another that hit the Letort Bridge on Louther St., as well as the cornerpost from a warehouse that stood on the corner of College and Main Sts. that was hit by a Confederate shell. A number of relics belonged to William Miller of Carlisle, who served in the 3rd Pennsylvania Cavalry and fought on the East Cavalry Battlefield at Gettysburg on July 3. Miller, who died in 1919, lost his sword during the battle. It was recovered—its tip broken—in 1881 and is now

Latrobe had not included a cupola in his original design, but the college fathers asked him to add one. He wanted to crown the cupola with a trident-shaped weathervane, but the local artisans translated his drawing into the somewhat odd and out-of-place mermaid that crowns Old West today (this is a replica; the original is in the college library). Over

on display here. The society is open Monday from 3 PM to 9 PM, Tuesday through Friday from 10 AM to 4 PM, and Saturday from 10 AM to 3 PM. There is no charge for admission. (717) 249-7610, www.historicalsociety.com.

The oldest surviving stone in **Carlisle's Old Public Graveyard**, S. Bedford and E. South Sts., dates from 1757, and it shares this space with some 750 veterans from the Revolutionary through the Korean Wars. About 550 are from the Civil War, including Charles Seebold, the drummer boy for the 1st U.S. Cavalry, who died on January 30, 1864, at the age of fourteen. It's also the burial spot of Mary Hays McCauly, better known as "Molly Pitcher" after her actions during the Revolutionary War's Battle of Monmouth. A statue of Molly and an iron cannon mark her grave today. The slate gravestone of William Blair, who died in 1802, has a hole made by a Confederate bullet. You can see the hole today, but be careful about probing it with your fingers—wasps have been known to build nests inside.

Many Civil War officers, North and South alike, were familiar with **Carlisle Barracks**, today home to the U.S. Army War College. The barracks was founded in 1757 and burned by Fitzhugh Lee in July 1863. It's open for visitors, but plan to go through security and produce a valid photo i.d., registration for your automobile, and proof of insurance. The barracks was also home to the Carlisle Federal Indian Boarding School from 1879 to 1918. Its most famous graduate was athlete Jim Thorpe. The school's intentions may have been good, but many today question the school's policy of stripping its pupils of their own national identities. Today the graves of 186 children who died while attending the school are in a small cemetery along the barracks fence on Claremont Rd. (717) 245-4773, carlislebarracks.carlisle.army.mil/sites/local.

The **Cumberland Valley Vistors Bureau** is at 18 N. Hanover St. in Carlisle, and its website is a good source for lodging and dining information, as well as a good resource about local attractions. www.visitcumberlandvalley.com.

the weekend of June 27 and 28, 1863, the mermaid overlooked a campus crowded with Confederate tents and campfires.

This first brush with the Rebels was a relatively peaceful one. Confederate officers who had been at the barracks made social calls, and many of them attended local churches on Sunday. According to one account, the pastor at the Lutheran Church had already chosen the 139th Psalm for his sermon. As he looked out at the Confederates filling the pews, he remembered that the psalm included the words, "Depart from me, therefore, ye bloody men." The Rebels didn't appear to take umbrage. Today the Lutheran Church is part of a complex on North Bedford Street that houses Bedford Street Antiques.

Ewell's stay was as brief as it was peaceful. On Monday he received orders from Robert E. Lee that the army was to converge near Gettysburg. "About three o'clock on Tuesday morning the rumbling of wagons announced a movement of the enemy," the *Carlisle American* reported. "Brigade after brigade passed until about eight o'clock the main army had disappeared." Carlisle breathed a sigh of relief, not only that the enemy soldiers had departed, but also that Ewell had done so little damage during his brief stay. "[W]ith the exception of the unavoidable litter and filth which attended his occupation of the position, no other damage was done." In fact, the paper reported, local civilians who plundered the barracks in the wake of the Rebels' departure caused more damage.

The relief was short lived. On July 1, Fitzhugh Lee and his brigade of Stuart's cavalry, exhausted after their long ride and their recent skirmish in Hanover, arrived on the outskirts of town, and instantly deflated the residents' sense of relief. "You cannot imagine the confusion that ensued," wrote seventeen-year-old Maggie Murray to her brother. "It was a disagreeable *surprise.*"

Union troops under Gen. William F. "Baldy" Smith (not to be confused with Confederate Gen. William "Extra Billy" Smith) had just reached town, and many of them were still sprawled around the main square, asleep or at rest, their arms stacked, when this new contingent of Rebels arrived. As the Federals scrambled to meet the threat, Lee sent in a messenger with a flag of truce demanding that the town surrender or he would shell it. Smith refused. Lee proved as good as his word.

James W. Sullivan was thirteen when the Rebels reached Carlisle. It was a time of great excitement for a boy, and then the shelling turned everything deadly serious. "The opening of the bombardment came like a series of rock blast explosions attended by aerial screams louder and more piercing than big siren rippers from industrial works," Sullivan remembered in a letter he wrote in 1932. "The three or four shots after the first followed one another so closely as to be almost simultaneous. One could imagine in action a battery, all the guns having awaited the

A monument in Carlisle's Veterans' Square honors those from Cumberland County who served the Union.

order to fire, going off at once. Thenceforth the reports came rather wide apart, at times up to half a minute."

Sullivan and his mother took shelter in a basement on Pitt Street next to the Methodist Church. They returned home to find their house had been hit. A heap of brick and stones littered the floor in front of the parlor fireplace, and mortar dust coated the room. "Mother's screams betrayed her fears that the house—her home for fifty years—was about to fall," Sullivan wrote. James went upstairs and discovered that the chimney had been smashed at garret level, and he realized that the debris downstairs had fallen down the chimney. Pieces of the shell still lay on the garret floor. Two other shells had passed completely through the roof without exploding. "The four holes in the shingles were as clean as though cut by carpenter tools."

Before Lee could do much more, he received an order from Stuart— who had changed course before reaching Carlisle to reunite with Lee— to move with all dispatch to Gettysburg. Once again, the Confederates headed south, leaving Carlisle to lick its wounds. The town had suffered no casualties during the brief shelling, but its residents' nerves had been shaken and their ire roused—ire aimed squarely at "this monster Lee." "If he should ever fall into the hands of Union soldiers, as we most devoutly hope he may, let mercy such as he showed, be meted out to him," said the *Carlisle American.*

Resentment still lingered in 1882, when a Carlisle resident wrote to Fitzhugh Lee and demanded to know why the Confederates had burned his lumberyard. "Now I have only time to say that it was with much regret I proceeded with hostile intent against Carlisle," Lee wrote. "My first military service after graduating from West Point was there. I knew & had received the hospitalities of most of its citizens. I had warm and earnest & good friends among its inhabitants. Some of the most pleasant days of my life was [*sic*] passed in the hospitable homes of her people—but war—horrid war—was raging then between them & those with me & my paths & their paths had separated."

Whether or not Lee's answer satisfied his questioner remains lost to history, but Carlisle's temper must have cooled by 1896, when Lee and Oliver O. Howard, the Union commander whose XI Corps had been routed by Stonewall Jackson at Chancellorsville and performed almost as badly at Gettysburg, shared the podium for the commencement exercises of the Carlisle Indian School.

Mechanicsburg

The Confederate infantry never made it much past Carlisle, but the cavalry under Jenkins, joined by some mounted infantry, continued to move north like the ocean foam ahead of a subsiding wave. Jenkins' mission was to scout Harrisburg's defenses and see if the capital was ripe for the plucking.

Mechanicsburg, previously known by the even less mellifluous names of Drytown, Stautterstown, and Pinchgut, was a small community of about 2,000 people when Jenkins and his 700 men arrived on June 28, 1863. Alerted to the Confederates' progress, many of the residents had already sent their goods out of town to keep them from Rebel hands. Jenkins waited on the outskirts and sent in a small scouting party. They rode to the house of Burgess George Hummel—still standing at 312 East Main Street—and ordered Mechanicsburg to surrender and give up the flag they had seen flying in the town square as they approached. The town had erected a new, 100-foot flagpole in the main square as a show of patriotism shortly after the war broke out, but as the Confederates approached, some citizens lowered the flag and brought it to the burgess for safekeeping. Lacking any means of defense, Hummel complied with the Rebel demands. The flag was last seen leaving town beneath a Rebel saddle.

Jenkins rode in once the town was secured. He perused the papers for war news at the Ashland House Hotel near the Cumberland Valley Railroad Station (now the American House Apartments at 26 North Market Street), and he ordered Burgess Hummel to provide rations and forage. "It was rather a novel spectacle in town, to see a large number of citizens wending their way to the Town Hall, on a Sabbath day, carrying baskets of provisions for a band of rebel invaders," noted the *Cumberland Valley Journal.* Then the Confederates moved further out of town.

Jenkins established his headquarters at the stone house of John Rupp on Trindle Springs Road, toward Harrisburg. The building is there today, at 5115 East Trindle Road, on a slight rise above busy Route 34. Jonas Rupp built the neatly mortared stone house in 1773, and his grandson John was living there as the Confederates approached. He opted not to greet them and fled to Lancaster instead. John Fenstermacher bought the house in 1997 and now uses it as the law offices for his firm, Fenstermacher and Associates. Fenstermacher was interested in antiques and the Civil War, but he knew nothing of the building's connection with Jenkins until after he purchased it.

A view of Mechanicsburg's main street from Frankeberger Tavern, the town's oldest building.

"It had been vacant for a long time," Fenstermacher says. "I'd always admired the building, but it was in bad shape." Previously the building had housed a restaurant, but when the owners departed, they left everything behind—not just the refrigerators, but even the stuff inside the refrigerators. "It took twenty tractor-trailer loads to get the trash out of here," says Fenstermacher.

From that uninspiring beginning, Fenstermacher turned the old Rupp house into a beautiful showcase, its restored interior now filled with antiques and Civil War memorabilia. In what used to be the old kitchen, Fenstermacher points out two beautiful corner cupboards made by Rupp family members. During the restoration, workers pulled up the old kitchen floorboards and found fragments of history—broken china, buttons, and a clay pipe. Fenstermacher keeps a sampling of the finds in a glass case on the second floor, including an imposing iron ax that may have been used by a blacksmith.

Jenkins gets his due outside, with a handsome granite monument that bears the general's bronze likeness. The Camp Curtin Historical Society placed the monument here in 2005.

A monument to Albert Jenkins stands outside the former home of John Rupp, where Jenkins set up headquarters in Mechanicsburg.

From his headquarters here, Jenkins made tentative attempts to probe Harrisburg' defenses. He set up some artillery near the Peace Church. Built in 1798 and used by a Lutheran and a Reformed congregation until 1866, the plain stone church stands now on a rise above busy Trindle Road, fighting a determined rear-guard defense against the march of time. The structure faces a gas station and a McDonald's across the street. From behind, traffic from Route 581 creates a dull roar, a marked contrast to the serenity of St. John's Cemetery, which butts up against the church's side. Stars stuck into the ground next to gravestones mark the resting places of Union veterans. There are also a plethora of Rupps buried here, including the former owners of Jenkins's headquarters.

Confederate cannon belied the Peace Church's name and threw shells in various directions in an attempt to flush out any hidden defenders. After some skirmishing along the Carlisle Pike, Confederate troops moved forward, reaching the vicinity of Oyster Point in White Hall (present-day Camp Hill). Oyster Point got its name because the Oyster family's tavern stood there at the spot where Trindle Spring Road and

Jenkins set up artillery at the 1798 Peace Church, near Mechanicsburg, during his brief venture to scout Harrisburg area defenses.

the Harrisburg-Carlisle Pike came together at a point. A historical marker on Market Street in Camp Hill marks the furthest point of the advance. There's not much about the leafy borough of Camp Hill today that suggests this was once a battlefield.

It's still leafy and pleasant up by the West Shore Country Club too, much as it probably was back in 1863 when William Henry Harrison Smith had a surprise encounter with the Rebels at his brother-in-law's house, located near modern Country Club Road. Smith, a Union soldier on furlough, was relaxing on the porch when Confederate scouts rode up. "They said, 'Yank, what are you doing here?'" Smith recalled; then they took him to see Jenkins.

Governor Curtin had issued a proclamation calling for volunteers on June 15, once the Southern invasion appeared imminent, but the response from Pennsylvanians had been tepid. The state did receive an infusion of 12,091 fighting men from New York, but in White Hall these bored militiamen ransacked houses and shops. "It seemed as if our soldiers thought they were in an enemy country," complained one local.

On June 29, the New Yorkers found another focus for their energies when Confederates again pushed forward toward Oyster Point, while Union artillery made a somewhat feeble defense—so feeble, in fact, that the guns did more damage to the Oyster Point Tavern by clipping it with a shell, than they did to the enemy. Confederate cannon added their own roar to the din. While his men occupied the Union troops, Jenkins made a personal reconnaissance of Harrisburg's defenses. He and some other officers from Ewell's headquarters rode as far as Drexel Hills above modern New Cumberland and gazed across the Susquehanna toward Harrisburg. They noted that the capital appeared to be poorly defended.

Ewell was prepared to spring upon Harrisburg, but then he received orders from Lee to fall back toward Gettysburg. It appears Ewell forgot to tell Jenkins, who remained far in advance in Mechanicsburg while the I Corps began moving south. Under the impression that the Rebels had all departed, on June 30 the 22nd and 37th New York militia and members of Landis's Philadelphia Brigade moved forward cautiously from Oyster Point. When they reached the Sporting Hill area, they received fire from Confederates hidden behind a barn. These were men under Col. Milton J. Ferguson, who were falling back from their position along Carlisle Pike and Orr's Bridge over Conodoguinet Creek. The skirmish is remembered as the Battle of Sporting Hill, com-

Mechanicsburg

The **Mechanicsburg Museum Association**, 2 Strawberry Alley (off Market St.), operates three buildings once used by the Cumberland Valley Railroad. The Association has a small museum in the old freight station, and the passenger station and stationmaster's house are also open for inspection. Museum hours are Tuesday through Saturday from noon to 3 PM. (717) 697-6088, www.mechanicsburgmuseum.org. The MMA also operates **Frankeberger Tavern**, 217 E. Main St., the oldest building in town. It started operating as a tavern in 1801. **Union Church**, 47 E. Main St., dates from 1825.

Jim Schmick's **Civil War and More**, 10 S. Market St., is just off the intersection where Market meets Main. The shop is open Monday through Friday from 11 AM to 6:30 PM and Saturday from 9 AM to 3 PM. (717) 766-1899 or (888) 444-1100, www.civilwarandmore.com.

It's not quite Civil War–era, but it's close. **Eckels Drugstore**, 36 E. Main St., opened in 1879. Eckels retains its old-fashioned feeling and is still a great place to get ice cream or a shake, or to browse through the small pharmacy museum. Scenes from the Winona Ryder movie *Girl Interrupted* were filmed here. It's open Thursday through Sunday from 11 AM on, until 9 PM in the summer and 5 PM in the winter. (717) 697-8404.

You can visit the Jenkins Memorial at the **Rupp House**, 5115 E. Trindle Rd. The house itself is a private office building. Further down Trindle Rd., the **Peace Church** appears like an apparition from the past from its perch above the intersections of Trindle and St. John's Church Rds. The Commonwealth acquired it in 1975. The simple interior contains many original items, including the nine-foot wineglass pulpit. Check out the keyboard on the 1807 organ—its keys are reversed (black keys are white and vice versa). Couples still hold weddings at the church, which also holds a service one Sunday a year. It's open to the public on Sundays from June through September from 2 PM to 5 PM. (717) 737-6492, www.historicpeacechurch.org.

memorated by a historical marker in the parking lot of Ye Olde Ale House on the Carlisle Pike.

In his 1965 account of the Pennsylvania campaign, *Here Come the Rebels*, Wilbur Sturtevant Nye described the setting as it was then, "a well-kept farming area with pastures, grainfields, small orchards around an occasional farmhouse, and here and there the great red barns so typical of the Pennsylvania-Dutch country." Time has marched on in the ensuing 140-plus years. The area around the historical marker is now a traffic-congested crossroads, with the overpasses of Route 581 snaking overhead just down the road. The only things that do battle at this busy intersection are the dueling drugstores on each side of the street, and the only maneuvers are carried out by drivers trying to get through the traffic lights before they change.

The two sides skirmished nearby throughout the afternoon until the arrival of Union artillery sent the Confederates retreating. The Rebels suffered perhaps sixteen dead and twenty to thirty wounded compared to eleven Union wounded. Never again would a Rebel army move this far north. The Battle of Sporting Hill was truly a true high-water mark for the Confederacy.

In 1938 an old man appeared in Camp Hill. He was a former Rebel soldier attending the 75th anniversary reunion at Gettysburg, and he wanted to see some old haunts. He told some neighborhood boys that he had scouted the area back in '63. To prove it, he told them to climb a tree on North 24th Street and find where he had carved his initials. True to his word, there they were.

pennsylvania
CIVIL WAR
TRAILS

Harrisburg
A Capital War

The Civil War never quite reached Harrisburg in 1863, although it came close enough to send the state capital into a panic. "All along the streets were omnibuses, wagons, and wheelbarrows taking in trunks and valuables and rushing them down to the depot to be shipped out of rebel range," wrote a reporter about the events in the city on June 16. "The scene at noon at the depots was indescribable, if not disgraceful. A sweltering mass of humanity thronged the platform, all furious to escape from the doomed city."

On the other side of the Susquehanna River, on a ridge called Hummel Heights in present-day Lemoyne, up to a thousand or more citizens eagerly pitched in to construct fortifications called Fort Washington. Their eagerness flagged by the second day, and so few returned to their labors that black railroad workers had to finish the job. Once Fort Washington was completed, Maj. Gen.

Maj. Gen. Darius Couch received command of the Department of the Susquehanna after the Union defeat at Chancellorsville. LIBRARY OF CONGRESS

Darius Couch, commander of the newly formed Department of the Susquehanna, realized the Rebels could render it useless by capturing a higher point of land to the west. Couch had another series of breastworks thrown up there. They were christened Fort Couch.

Traces of Fort Couch remain in Lemoyne. A beautiful granite memorial, placed there by the Camp Curtin Historical Society in 2005, marks the site in a little park by a big water tower, and the sinuous entrenchments are plainly visible. In 1863, when the community was called Bridgeport, this was farmland. Today this portion of Lemoyne is a residential neighborhood, with steep roads and curving streets that make it feel more like California than Pennsylvania. Nearby is Negley Park, which offers tremendous views of Harrisburg and is a popular spot for people to watch Fourth of July fireworks displays.

In a sense, the Civil War finally reached Harrisburg on Lincoln's birthday in 2001, the day that The National Civil War Museum opened in the city's Reservoir Park, on a hilltop with sweeping views of the capital city and the Susquehanna River Valley.

The goal of its founder, Harrisburg mayor Stephen R. Reed, was the creation of a museum that would tell the story of the entire Civil War, without bias toward North or South. "We want Americans to know and understand the Civil War because we believe that allows them to better understand the society in which we now live," he explains from behind his desk in his office downtown. Reed believed such a museum would be good for Harrisburg—one of the most economically distressed cities in the nation when he became mayor in 1980—and he felt that Harrisburg was the perfect place for such a museum. "Harrisburg, next to Gettysburg, was the second-most important place during the Civil War in Pennsylvania," he says. It was an important rail center, it was the site of Camp Curtin, the largest training camp during the war, and it was one of the military objectives of Robert E. Lee's two northern campaigns.

Reed also wanted the museum to take an unblinking look at slavery. "How could you tell the story of the American Civil War and leave out slavery," he asks.

The museum's slavery exhibits have an undeniable power. There is something sobering about the sight of shackles and whips when you understand the gritty reality of their employment, but the museum also uses realistic mannequins to recreate a slave auction, with the mother

Moment of Mercy stands in front of the National Civil War Museum in Harrisburg and commemorates an incident from the Battle of Fredericksburg.

weeping as her children are sold away from her. Nearby, another figure in a slave jail glares balefully through the bars. Schoolchildren sometimes step back nervously when they catch his gaze.

From the exhibits about slavery and other forces leading to war, visitors pass a large recreation of Fort Sumter's battlements. There's a large gallery devoted to Gettysburg, and a gruesomely realistic recreation of a Civil War surgeon at work. As visitors wind their way through the galleries, a series of flat-screen TVs tell the story of several fictionalized characters as they make their own way through the war.

And of course there are artifacts. Among Reed's purchases: a large collection of items connected with Confederate general George Pickett of "Pickett's Charge" fame, two of Jeb Stuart's sabers, and a multitude of guns, canteens, ordinance, uniforms, camp equipment, musical instruments, and other artifacts. You can see one of the gauntlets Stonewall Jackson was wearing when he was mortally wounded by his own troops at Chancellorsville; Robert E. Lee's Bible, captured on a supply wagon before Appomattox; Abraham Lincoln's hatbox; and a saddle George McClellan used.

The items on display are only about one-third of the collection. The rest remain behind locked doors in a secure storage room, out of public view, except when curator Brett Kelley takes small groups of museum members on tours. Kelley is a former Marine who began working for the museum in 1999, even before it opened. One thing he discovered after he began work here was that he has a personal connection to the Civil War—his great-great grandfather served in the 2nd Vermont Infantry. During his tours of the storage facility, Kelley shows actual battle maps that Robert E. Lee used during the war's final days, and the framed commission of Union Gen. John Sedgwick, signed

Artifacts from The National Civil War Museum collection: Robert E. Lee's Bible and gauntlets that were in his possession throughout the war.

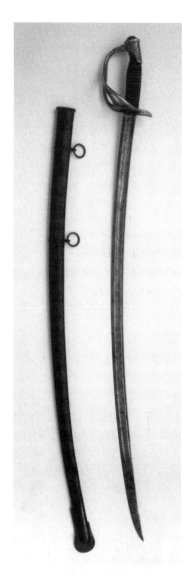

J. E. B. Stuart's saber and scabbard from The National Civil War Museum collection.
THE NATIONAL CIVIL WAR MUSEUM

by Abraham Lincoln and Secretary of War Edwin Stanton. There are shelves and racks that hold uniforms, flags, writing desks, ordnance—practically everything you'd need to fight another Civil War.

A bank of gray metal drawers holds an incredible variety of smaller items, everything from uniform buttons and medals to soap. There are inkwells and drafting instruments, envelopes and pencils, even two minié balls that fused together when they collided in flight. Kelley removes a small wooden cabinet that contains a lock of Lincoln's hair. From an envelope he carefully takes out Robert E. Lee's bookmark, taken from his Arlington house by a Union soldier. Like the artifacts of the saints that early Christians used to worship, these are truly relics of the Civil War.

There are more relics in another Civil War museum in Harrisburg, but relatively few people know about them. From the outside, the Civil War Flag Conservation Facility's building is drab and decrepit. Inside, 390 of the state's Civil War flags and 22 more from the Spanish-American War lie in large cabinets draped with white protective covers inside a modern temperature- and humidity-controlled room. Until they arrived here in 1985, many of them were deteriorating in glass cases inside the Capitol rotunda.

Flags played important roles during the Civil War, and not merely as stirring symbols. The movement of the flags on the battlefield allowed commanders to follow the fighting's ebb and flow. The banners also served as rallying points for the troops. "I liken them to the radio transmissions of the time," says Jason Wilson, the research historian for the Pennsylvania Capitol Preservation Committee, the agency in charge of the facility. "Wherever the flag was going, that's what the regiment was doing." The color bearers—the men who carried the flags—had a position of honor. There are many stories of bearers who threw up heroic resistance to keep their flags from falling into enemy hands—or even the hands of their own officers. When Brig. Gen. Samuel Crawford, out in the Wheatfield at Gettysburg, grabbed the flag of the 1st Pennsylvania Reserves to rally his troops, the bearer didn't want to give it up. "The general reminded him who he was, and said he was just borrowing the flag for a moment," Wilson says. As Crawford rode forward, the color bearer trotted alongside his horse until he got the flag back.

Wilson is a color bearer of sorts himself. One of his charges, which he's pulled out from its cabinet on a drawer, like a specimen on a mortuary slab, is the regimental flag from the 83rd Pennsylvania. Somewhat tattered, it's a square, thirty-four-star banner, modeled on the U.S. flag, but with the Pennsylvania coat of arms in the canton, or blue field. "This would have been on Little Round Top on the second day at Gettysburg," Wilson says. The 83rd was serving in a cobbled-together brigade under its former commander, Col. Strong Vincent. On July 2, Vincent intercepted a courier bearing a message that said troops were needed to defend the Round Tops. Vincent took the responsibility upon himself and led his troops—the 20th Maine, the 83rd Pennsylvania, the 44th New York, and the 16th Michigan—to Little Round Top, where they arrived just in time to successfully defend the important position from Confederate attack. Vincent himself was mortally wounded during the fighting.

Age alone isn't responsible for the damage to the flag from the 97th Pennsylvania. "Every hole you see in here is a bullet hole," Wilson says. "It was part of the attack on Fort Fisher in Wilmington, North Carolina, in 1865." During the battle, Col. Galusha Pennypacker grabbed the flag and used it to rally his troops on top of the fort. Pennypacker, who had grown up in the house at Valley Forge that George Washington used as his headquarters, received four wounds on the fort's ramparts. "He refused to be moved until the engagement was decided," says Wilson. The flag's color sergeant later reported that the flag was hit 101 times.

Harrisburg

You can find what remains of **Fort Couch**, 8th St. and Indiana Ave., in Lemoyne. The Camp Curtin Historical Society erected the handsome memorial to Darius Couch and the fort here in 2005.

The view alone is worth a visit to Harrisburg's **National Civil War Museum**, 1 Lincoln Circle, but make sure you go inside too. The museum is in Reservoir Park, overlooking the city. It's open Monday through Saturday from 10 AM to 5 PM, and Sunday and select holidays from noon until 5 PM. It's closed Mondays and Tuesdays between Labor Day and March 31. There is an admission charge. (717) 260-1861 or (866) BLUE-GRAY, www.national civilwarmuseum.org.

You can see flags, flags, and more flags at the **Civil War Flag Conservation Facility**, 10th and Market Sts., but you must call ahead for an appointment first. (717) 783-6484, cpc.state.pa.us/main/cpcweb/projects/preserv civwartreasure.html.

The **John Harris-Simon Cameron Mansion**, 219 S. Front St., is also the headquarters of the Historical Society of Dauphin County. Just across busy Front Street (cross with caution!) is the gravesite of Harrisburg's founder, John Harris Jr. The society's office hours are Monday through Thursday 9:30 AM to 4 PM. The mansion is open for tours by appointment only. There is a fee. (717) 233-3462, www.dauphincountyhistoricalsociety.org.

There are 155 Civil War graves at **Harrisburg Cemetery**, 13th and Liberty sts. It's also the last resting place of Maj. Gen. Andrew Porter, who was Mary Todd Lincoln's great-grandfather. Porter fought in the Revolutionary War as an aide to George Washington. (717) 234-8661. **Lincoln Cemetery** is at the intersection of 30th St. and Boosler Ave., in Penbrook. The Afrolumens Project has much information about the cemetery on its website, www.afrolumens. org/rising_free/lincoln/lincmain.html. Other black soldiers are buried in Steelton at **Midland Cemetery**, Cole Alley. www.afrolumens.org/rising_free/friends.html.

A statue of Governor **Andrew Gregg Curtin** stands at the site of the Civil War camp named after him, 6th and Woodbine Sts. Next to it is Camp Curtin Memorial–Mitchell United Methodist Church, 2221 Sixth St., which includes a stained-glass window that depicts a Civil War soldier.

The **Camp Curtin Historical Society and Civil War Round Table** is a nonprofit organization that seeks to preserve the history of Camp Curtin. It holds quarterly meetings, sponsors tours, and issues a newsletter. For more about membership, contact the society at 2221 N. Sixth St., Harrisburg, PA 17110. (717) 233-0335, www.campcurtin.org.

The 110-foot-tall obelisk of the **Dauphin County Memorial**, Third and Division Sts., honors the men from the county who served in the "War for the Suppression of the Rebellion." Erected in 1869 in front of the Capitol, it was moved here in 1959.

Housed in a distinctive round building next to the Capitol, **The State Museum of Pennsylvania**, 300 North St., includes exhibits on all aspects of Pennsylvania history, including a newly revamped Civil War room. The main attraction is Peter Rothermel's huge painting of the Battle of Gettysburg, a colossal 16-x-32 canvas that captures the events at the battle's high-water mark. The museum's hours are Tuesday through Saturday 9 AM to 5 PM, and Sunday noon to 5 PM. Admission is free. (717) 787-4980, www.statemuseum pa.org. The tall building next door is the **Pennsylvania State Archives**, Third and Forster Sts., which houses many Pennsylvania-related Civil War documents. Among them are the state's Civil War muster rolls, currently in the midst of a $1.1 million conservation project. (717) 783-3281, www.phmc.state.pa.us.

Behind the Capitol in **Soldiers Grove**, Commonwealth Ave. and State St., is the state's Medal of Honor Memorial, which lists the names of each recipient, including those from the Civil War. A historical marker here also commemorates the United States Colored Troops Grand Review, which started here on November 14, 1865. (Black troops were not allowed to march in the much larger Grand Review march in Washington, D.C.) Speakers for the event included Simon Cameron and T. Morris Chester. On the grounds on the other side of the Capitol is the **John Frederick Hartranft** statue. Hartranft served throughout the war, from First Manassas (where he earned the Medal of Honor, even though his men, their terms of service up, left before the battle) through the final campaigns against Robert E. Lee. After the war, he served as special provost marshall for the trial of the Lincoln conspirators, and as a two-term governor of Pennsylvania.

The original stone portion of the **Broad Street Market**, 1233 N. Third St., dates from 1860. Soldiers from Camp Curtin stopped here; you can too. It's open Thursday and Friday from 7 AM to 5 PM, and Saturday from 7 AM to 4 PM (717) 236-7923.

For his heroics at Fort Fisher, Pennypacker received the Medal of Honor. He also became the youngest general of the war, beating out George Custer when he received his promotion before he turned twenty-one.

Flagstaffs are in separate cabinets. One stands out from the pack, because it has a deer tail attached to the top. This is the staff from the 42nd Pennsylvania—the Bucktails. Originally called the 13th Pennsylvania Reserves, this unit of sharpshooting hunters wore deer tails on their hats and earned a reputation for their fighting on the battlefield and their rowdy behavior off it. One night in May 1861, when the Bucktails were still at Camp Curtin in Harrisburg, a policeman tried to arrest one of them who was drunk on the streets. The resulting riot required three companies of men to rush in from the camp to quiet things down.

The flag that would have been attached to this staff recently ended a long exodus from Pennsylvania, returning in 2003 after a lengthy stay at the Smithsonian Institution in Washington. Today the banner is laid out on a table. It will obviously require a lot of work. Much of the flag is in tatters. A big piece is missing from the coat of arms in the canton, and several of the stripes look like one of the Dead Sea Scrolls, little more than fragments of fabric laid out in the proper position. Pieces of weighed glass flatten other portions of the flag.

"This flag was actually captured on the Peninsula campaign in 1862," Wilson says. The regiment was surrounded, so they buried the flag in White Oak Swamp rather than risk having the Confederates capture it. Apparently they didn't dig deep enough. After Richmond fell in April 1865, the flag was found in the Confederate Capitol and removed by the unit's original commander, Edward Ord. When Ord died, his daughter gave the flag to the Smithsonian as a permanent loan. And there it remained, where it fell behind a drawer and suffered much damage, until a group who portrayed the Bucktails at reenactments successfully lobbied for its return to Pennsylvania. Wilson says the flag will be humidified to restore the fabric's pliability, and then a covering will be sewn over it. It won't be perfect, but at least it will survive.

One evening, Jim Schmick gives a presentation at the Harris/Cameron mansion, the headquarters of the Historical Society of Dauphin County. Schmick works as a postman during the day, but the Civil War is his passion, one sparked by childhood visits to Gettysburg. He founded the Camp Curtin Historical Society and Civil War Roundtable, and he owns and operates Civil War and More, a shop in Mechanicsburg. Tonight, a standing-room-only audience sits on metal folding chairs as Schmick clicks through a slide presentation of Civil War sites in Harrisburg. He starts with a photo of two-year-old Jim Schmick astride a cannon at Gettysburg, then moves through period engravings, photographs of the buildings that occupy historic sites today, and even a cigar box that honored local Civil War hero John Frederick Hartranft, whose equestrian statue stands on the Capitol grounds. He runs through about 140 slides in an efficient forty-five minutes. "The hard-core presentation has 300 slides and takes three and a half hours, with a fifteen-minute break," he says afterward.

His venue is a Civil War landmark in its own right. John Harris Jr., Harrisburg's founder, constructed the building out of local limestone around 1766. Simon Cameron, Lincoln's first secretary of war, bought the house in 1863, and he lived here until his death twenty-six years later.

A thin-faced, thin-lipped man, Cameron had been born into poverty in Lancaster, became a printer, and bought a Harrisburg newspaper, the *Republican*, in 1826. In the state capital he began actively clutching at the levers of power, backing rising politician James Buchanan and launching a reputation for corruption that dogged him to the end of his days. Cameron's enemies called him "Winnebago Chief" because he supposedly swindled an Indian tribe. "He always took advantage of loopholes and that sort of thing," says Bob Hill, director of collections for the Historical Society of Dauphin County. "He didn't violate laws, but some of his actions were questionable."

Cameron served in the Senate, and he earned a position as secretary of war by backing Abraham Lincoln at the 1860 Republican convention. Lincoln told his advisors not to cut deals, and he wasn't pleased when they cut one with the wily Pennsylvanian. Cameron wanted the treasury department, but he settled for the position of secretary of war. "Cameron figured it could be every bit as lucrative," says Hill. "Perhaps more so." In fact, for a man with an itch for self enrichment, it was ideal. Chaos bred opportunity, and Cameron's opponents charged that the new secretary sold the government poor-quality guns and mules and that he unfairly favored his fellow Pennsylvanians for jobs and contracts. Cameron's reputation for corruption and inefficiency finally forced Lincoln to send him into exile—all the way to Russia, where he served briefly as minister.

"Ugh! ugh! Send word to the Czar to bring in his things of nights," one senator wrote regarding the Winnebago Chief's appointment.

When he returned to Harrisburg in 1863, Cameron purchased the Harris place and turned it into a home suited for a person of his position. In France he had purchased two fourteen-foot mirrors, and the only way he could fit them into his new mansion was by lowering the ground-level floors three feet. The mansion still provides a setting of opulent splendor and includes many of Cameron's own furnishings, including the mirrors, fireplaces made of Italian marble, and windows of Bavarian cobalt glass in the alcove off the parlor. A life-size portrait of Cameron adorns the wall next to one of the fireplaces. In it he stands with a walking stick in one hand, his coat thrown jauntily over the crook of his left arm. But the impression of elegance is diminished by the pinched expression on Cameron's face. He looks like he's dressed for a ball, but can't stop thinking of new ways to cook the books.

When Cameron died in 1889, he didn't travel far from his mansion. He now rests in the family plot in Harrisburg Cemetery. Separated from downtown Harrisburg by rail lines, the cemetery seems to exist in a realm of its own. Drive through the gates and you leave Harrisburg's urban bustle behind and enter a world of peace and quiet, where flowering trees are in bloom, birds chirp, and all is pastoral and serene. It's a good advertisement for the afterlife.

The cemetery has many Civil War connections. For example, John White Geary lies on a hillside facing town. His bronze likeness stands beneath the spreading branches of a huge oak, a bronze hat—adorned with bronze acorns on the rim—held at his side in one bronze hand.

Geary's career ranged across the breadth of the United States. He served as San Francisco's first mayor. He was territorial governor of Kansas when that region was embroiled by the tumultuous debate over

After a career that spanned the continent, John W. Geary served as a general in the Civil War and later as governor of Pennsylvania. LIBRARY OF CONGRESS

whether it should be free or slave. Geary was anti-slavery and soon resigned. As a soldier he fought in the Mexican War, and when the Civil War broke out, Geary raised the 28th Pennsylvania Volunteer Infantry and fought well and bravely at Cedar Mountain, Chancellorsville, Gettysburg, Chattanooga, and with Gen. William T. Sherman in Georgia. Geary was balding on top, but had a luxuriant, Old Testament prophet's beard as though to compensate. Historian Stephen Sears called him "a fearless giant of a man who led by example." Geary ended the war as a major general and later served two terms as Pennsylvania's governor. He died in 1873.

A double line of small stones near the rear mark the graves of less exalted personages. Several of them are Confederate soldiers who died in area hospitals or prison camps. Their stones are thicker than the

The gravestones of the Confederate soldiers in Harrisburg Cemetery have pointed tops to distinguish them from the rounded-top Union stones.

Union ones, and instead of being rounded, they come to a point on top—to prevent Yankees from sitting on them, legend says. The irony is that the thin limestone gravestones of the Yankee soldiers have all weathered into illegibility, while you can still read the names on the Confederate stones.

There's another irony here. The city was willing to bury Confederate soldiers in Harrisburg Cemetery, but African Americans had to look elsewhere—many of them in Lincoln Cemetery across town.

Calobe Jackson Jr., retired postman and Harrisburg native, takes an active interest in Lincoln Cemetery and has learned a great deal about the people buried there since he retired in 1989. "I'd heard a lot of stories in my dad's barbershop," says Jackson, age seventy-six. "I found out that most of them were true." He points out the gravestone of Jacob Cumpton, who reportedly drove the carriage that took Abraham Lincoln to his train on February 22, 1861. Lincoln was in Harrisburg on his way to Washington for his inauguration when he made a hasty and secret departure under an assassination threat. Cumpton later served as a soldier in the war.

Jackson has a personal link with two of the veterans buried here, John Henry Barton, who died in 1942, and Ephraim Slaughter, who was Dauphin County's last surviving Civil War veteran when he died a year later. Jackson remembers seeing both men in Harrisburg's Memorial Day parade in 1942. "They had them in convertibles coming across the Soldiers and Sailors Bridge," Jackson says. "And they led the parade."

Lincoln Cemetery also contains the grave of Harrisburg native Thomas Morris Chester. His mother had escaped from slavery in Maryland and married a local man. Son Thomas, one of twelve children, was educated at the Allegheny Institute outside Pittsburgh. He wanted to study law, but lacked the money. Instead, he became involved in the movement to colonize the African country of Liberia with former American slaves, and even lived in Liberia himself for a time. During the Civil War Chester devoted his energies to raising regiments of black soldiers for the Union, and he wrote for the Philadelphia *Press*, the only black correspondent for a major white paper. He submitted articles about African American fighting men, and he covered the fall of Richmond. After the war, Chester practiced law in England and New Orleans. He died in Harrisburg in 1892.

Born in Harrisburg, Thomas Morris Chester raised black troops for the Union and served as a war correspondent.
UNIVERSITY ARCHIVES, CHEYNEY UNIVERSITY OF PENNSYLVANIA

Chester's gravestone here in Lincoln Cemetery is small. It also had his birth date incorrect. That was changed in 2002 when the original stone was raised and placed on top of a new stone with the correct date. It's still small in comparison to that of his younger brother David, which stands next in line. David had moved to Philadelphia, where he became the second black man to serve on the city council. He died while in office, and the Philadelphia city council paid for his large gravestone.

Wartime governor Andrew Curtin isn't buried in Harrisburg—his grave is in his hometown of Bellefonte—but you can find a statue of the governor on the site of the training camp that bore his name. Camp Curtin, Harrisburg's most important contribution to the Union cause, marked the first step on the road to war for many of the state's Civil War veterans. More than 300,000 soldiers passed through the camp before heading off to fight. Many of them passed through again to be discharged from the army.

Little remains to remind people of Camp Curtin today. Governor Curtin's statue, dedicated in 1922, stands at the corner of Sixth and Woodbine streets in the city's uptown district, next to Camp Curtin Memorial–Mitchell United Methodist Church and across Woodbine Street from the Camp Curtin YMCA.

That's perhaps an inadequate memorial to Curtin, who played a key role in the preservation of the Union, but it used to be worse. In 1989 Jim Schmick attended a talk about Camp Curtin and learned that the monument was just a few blocks off his mail route. He went to see it and found the statue defaced by graffiti and paint, and the little park surrounding it shabby and derelict. "It was pretty bad," he says. Schmick began making inquires about the statue and the state eventually offered some money to restore it. On November 11, 1990, Curtin's great-great-grandson participated in a ceremony to unveil the restored monument.

Curtin's statue stands in a tiny park in a somewhat run-down neighborhood, but there was a time when this land lay outside Harrisburg. When Brig. Gen. Edward C. William, commander of the state's militia, and Maj. Joseph Knipe, a native of Mount Joy, a veteran of the Mexican War, and William's aide, began looking for a site where they could gather Pennsylvania's soldiers, they picked eighty acres of land about a mile north of Harrisburg on Dauphin County's Agricultural Fairgrounds. On April 18, 1861, Knipe raised the American flag over the new camp and proposed that it be named after the governor. The camp was initially a camp of rendezvous, a place where men were organized into companies and regiments. Only later did it become a camp of training, where green soldiers would learn the discipline necessary for military life.

The camp's population constantly ebbed and flowed. At times, it was nearly deserted. Other times, when new units were brought in, it bustled. Confederate prisoners passed through on their way to permanent prisons, and wounded soldiers recuperated or died in the camp hospital.

Camp Curtin saw one last flood of soldiers when men were mustered out of the army after the war ended. By June 1865, the camp's 7,000 soldiers spilled over into an annex called Camp Return. With so many bored men in the region, the provost marshal ordered all of Harrisburg's drinking establishments closed. As the summer of 1865 dissolved into fall, the flood of discharged soldiers slowed to a trickle. On November 11, 1865, Camp Curtin officially closed.

Around that time Governor Curtin spoke to a gathering of Civil War veterans at the camp. "The field upon which we now stand will be known as classic ground, for here has been the great central point of the organization of our military forces," he said. "When my administration of public affairs will have been forgotten, and the good and evil will be only known to the investigation of the antiquarian, Camp Curtin, with its memories and associations will be immortal." Curtin was correct on the first count but wrong on the second one. Neither his administration nor the camp named after him are much remembered, except among Civil War buffs and historians. But Curtin's statue still stands on the site of the camp that bore his name, in the city where he did so much to help the Union cause.

★ pennsylvania ★
**CIVIL WAR
TRAILS**

York
Divided and Conquered

In 1863, Confederate soldiers occupied the capital of the United States. Not Washington, D.C., which remained nervous but safe. Instead, the Rebels marched into York, Pennsylvania. The southern Pennsylvania town had briefly served as the capital of the fledgling nation in 1777 and 1778 during the Revolutionary War, when the British captured Philadelphia and drove the Continental Congress farther west into Pennsylvania. Congress adopted the Articles of Confederation in York, and the city today proudly remembers its Revolutionary War history with a number of historical markers, as well as the Colonial Complex of period buildings downtown.

York's Civil War history, though, is another matter. On July 28, 1863, the Confederates lowered the American flag in York's public square after the city sur-

Fiery and profane, Maj. Gen. Jubal Early threatened to burn York if the city didn't pay a $100,000 ransom.
LIBRARY OF CONGRESS

67

rendered to Rebel forces under Maj. Gen. Jubal Early. York became the largest northern city to be occupied by enemy forces.

Richard Banz, the director of interpretation and collections for the York County Heritage Trust, says the city remains somewhat reluctant to take a hard look at the fact of its occupation by the enemy. That was a common experience for cities in the South, he points out, but not in the North. "In the South they've dealt with it," Banz says. "It's harder to deal with when you're north of the Mason-Dixon line."

It was even harder to deal with in 1863. "Men who don't often weep, wept then," wrote resident Cassandra Small.

Few weep about it now, and during York's annual Patriot Days event in June, the city even produces an outdoor performance of "The Confederate Occupation of York: A Drama," a short play written by resident Scott Butcher. Relying on contemporary sources and the words of principals themselves, the play tells the story of the events of June 1863. Butcher plays Confederate Brig. Gen. John B. Gordon. Richard Banz, his beard chopped back to mutton chops, takes on the role of Maj. Granville O. Haller, the York native charged with defending the city who was later kicked out of the army for "disloyal conduct, and the utterance of disloyal sentiments." C. Edward LeFevre of Manheim plays Confederate general William "Extra Billy" Smith with panache. He even carries a blue umbrella, just as the real general did. The play unfolds on the steps of the York County Courthouse, a building that dates from 1898, but retains elements from the courthouse that stood on this site when the Confederates came to town.

On Saturday, June 27, as the city waited in trepidation to see what the invaders would do, York businessman Arthur Briggs Farquhar launched his own personal diplomatic mission. "I hitched a buggy and went to meet the Confederate army on my own," he recalled. He found the Confederates about ten miles outside town at the farm of Jacob S. Altland. Farquhar had attended school in Virginia and knew one of the officers, who brought him to General Gordon. "He appeared happy to make any arrangements he could to save the citizens of York from hardship and jotted down on a piece of paper a note that nothing in the town would be harmed if they honored his requisitions for supplies," Farquhar wrote. Later that day, a five-man Committee of Safety arrived from York to negotiate further with the General. If he promised not to burn the town, they said, they promised the town would not resist the Confederates.

Maj. Granville Haller moved his troops out of York and offered his services to the defense of Wrightsville.
ADAMS COUNTY HISTORICAL SOCIETY

The committee asked Granville Haller to take his men and leave town. The Confederates had already driven Haller out of Gettysburg two days earlier. Now they were pushing him out of York, even though he said he was prepared to offer resistance. "This movement was not appreciated by the citizens, who, apprehensive that a collision might subject the town to the vengeance of the enemy, believed it would do the inhabitants much injury," said Haller, who took his 350 men and headed east to Wrightsville.

Gordon's men rode into York on Sunday morning and pulled down an American flag that was flying from a tall flagpole in the main square. "Extra Billy" Smith arrived with his brigade shortly afterward. Smith was another of the Confederacy's quirky personalities. He was a politician who had earned his nickname because of the money the post office gave him for running a coach service from Washington, D.C., to Georgia. Smith, who would turn sixty-six that September, had already served as a state senator, U.S. congressman, and governor of Virginia. "As a soldier he was equally distinguished for personal intrepidity and contempt for what he called 'tactics' and for educated and trained soldiers, whom he was wont to speak of as 'those West P'int fellows,'" remembered Maj. Robert Stiles, an artilleryman from Georgia.

Smith and his men rode into York as church bells rang on a beautiful sunny Sunday. Churchgoers thronged the streets in their Sunday best, and Smith bowed this way and that as he made his way through town. The reception, in fact, moved him to oratory when he reached the central square. "My friends, how do you like this way of coming back into the Union?" he asked the gathered citizens. "I hope you like it; I have been in favor of it for a good while." Smith appeared to be enjoying himself, and according to the Robert Stiles account, the people of York enjoyed the performance as well. "Are we not a fine set of fellows?" Smith asked them. "You must admit that we are."

One man who remained unamused was Smith's division commander, Jubal Early, who reached town behind Extra Billy. Forced to make his

From her father's home on Market Street, Cassandra Small wrote her cousin a detailed description of the Confederate occupation of York. YORK COUNTY HERITAGE TRUST

way through the crowd, the dyspeptic Early was quickly aroused to full temper. "General Smith, what the devil are you about?" he demanded.

Smith remained unfazed. "Having a little fun, General," he replied, "which is good for all of us, and at the same time teaching these people something that will be good for them and won't do us any harm."

Cassandra Small, the daughter of prominent businessman Philip Small, wrote her cousin Lissie in Baltimore a detailed account of the Confederates' arrival. She lived at her father's house on the corner of Market and Duke streets, a classical brick building that now provides a home for business and social organization called the Lafayette Club. Cassandra also had a personal connection with the invaders—a cousin, George Latimer, was a member of Gordon's brigade. "[H]appily we didn't see him, as we should not have spoken to him," she noted.

"Sunday morning Mother, Mary and I, dressed for church; all the rest expected to stay at home," Small wrote. "Just as the bells rang, the cry was heard, 'They are coming!' Oh, Lissy, what did we feel like? Humiliated! disgraced! Men who don't often weep, wept then. They came with loud music, flags flying. First we saw a picket in front of our door. Where he came from or how he got there, no one knew, he came so suddenly and quietly (other pickets were all along the street). When we spoke to him, he said they were only to keep the men in line."

Later, General Gordon himself made an appearance in front of the Small residence. "'Ladies, I have a word to say,'" Small recounted Gordon saying. "'I suppose you think me a pretty rough looking man, but when I am shaved and dressed, my wife considers me a very good looking fellow. I want to say to you we have not come among you to pursue the same warfare your men did in our country. You need not have any fear of us, whilst we are in your midst. You are just as safe as though we were a thousand miles away. That is all I have to say.' He bowed and turning his horse rode away."

Gordon and his brigade were soon on his way east toward Wrightsville and the bridge that spanned the Susquehanna there, while Early remained behind and made demands on York. He requested shoes, hats, rations—and $100,000 in greenbacks to keep him from burning the town. York could raise only $28,600, but Chief Burgess David Small talked Early out of burning railroad equipment in reprisal. Early never got the chance to squeeze the rest of the sum from York before he received orders to bring his division to Gettysburg. "Well, they have gone—I hope never to return," Small wrote her cousin. "May the Lord preserve us from such distress again."

After the performance of the play on the courthouse steps, Banz and Butcher remain in uniform—Banz as Haller and Butcher as Gordon—to guide a walking tour of York's historic district. The two men engage in good-natured banter as they lead the tour group past the buildings and down the streets that witnessed the arrival of the Confederates.

Banz talks a little about Haller's career. The York native had tried to get an appointment to West Point, but then-Senator James Buchanan named another York native, William Buell Franklin, instead. (Franklin, whose reputation suffered a severe blow after the Battle of Fredericksburg in Virginia, is buried in York's Prospect Hill Cemetery.) Denied the West Point education that would have cleared his path toward promotion, Haller soldiered on in the regular army. He fought in the Indian wars out West and distinguished himself in Mexico. During the first part of the Civil War, Haller commanded Maj. Gen. George McClellan's headquarters guard. Remarks he made after the disastrous Union defeat at Fredericksburg led to an investigation and eventually to his expulsion from the army. Haller headed back West, where he became a prominent, and rich, citizen of Seattle. Years later a court of inquiry cleared Haller's name, and he died a respectable death in Seattle in 1897.

While in York, Brig. Gen. John B. Gordon received a mysterious message about the defenses in Wrightsville.
LIBRARY OF CONGRESS

York

The **Downtown York Visitors Information Center**, 155 W. Market St., is a good place to start your visit. It's open daily from 9:30 AM to 4 PM. (717) 852-9675, www.yorkpa.org.

The 1921 building that houses the **York County Heritage Trust**, 250 E. Market St., used to be a car dealership. Now it's filled with artifacts and exhibits that detail area history. The Civil War room includes weapons, flags, portraits, and even a re-creation of the sitting room where Cassandra Small wrote to her cousin about the Confederate occupation. "A Picturesque Looking Glass: The Drawings of Lewis Miller" displays the folk illustrations of Miller (1796–1882), a local man whose colorful work captured the York he knew, including the arrival of the Confederates. The museum is open Tuesday through Saturday from 10 AM to 4 PM. The library is open Tuesday through Saturday from 10 AM to 4 PM. There is an admission charge for the museum, which includes admission to all the trust's properties in town. (717) 848-1587, www.yorkheritage.org.

The trust's other properties include the Victorian-era **Bonham House**, 152 E. Market St. It's open Saturday from 10 AM to 4 PM. **The Colonial Complex**, 157 W. Market St., comprises the Gates House, the Plough Tavern, the Bobb Log House, and the Colonial Court House. It's open Tuesday through

The tour stops in front of a modest brick townhouse on Philadelphia Street that once belonged to William Goodridge. The building is being renovated to reopen as an Underground Railroad museum, and the location is more than fitting, because Goodridge, a former slave himself, played an active role helping escaped slaves towards freedom. As a barber in York, Goodridge amassed a substantial sum through various business interests and real estate investment. At one point he owned twenty properties in town, including York's tallest building, a five-story structure on the central square. Goodridge also had a literal railroad business, operating thirteen rail cars as the Goodridge Reliance Line, which he sometimes used to smuggle slaves out of York. When Civil War broke out, Goodridge realized that York, a county that bordered the slave state of Maryland, was growing increasingly unsafe. He left Penn-

Saturday from 10 AM to 4 PM. (717) 845-2951. The **Fire Museum of York County**, 757 W. Market St., is open Saturday from 10 AM to 4 PM. The **Agricultural and Industrial Museum**, 217 W. Princess St., includes everything from antique cars to a recreated grist mill, complete with water wheel. Its hours are Tuesday through Saturday from 10 AM to 4 PM. (717) 846-6452.

The sixty-five-foot **Soldiers and Sailors Monument**, Penn Park, stands on the site of a Union hospital that opened on June 18, 1862. During the war, more than 14,000 people were treated there, including wounded from Hanover and Gettysburg.

More than a thousand Civil War soldiers are buried at **Prospect Hill Cemetery**, 700 N. George St. Many of the soldiers who died at the hospital at Penn Common were buried here at Soldiers Circle. David Small, York's burgess during the occupation, is buried here too, as are Arthur Briggs Farquhar and Cassandra Small and her husband, Dr. Alexander R. Blair, who was a surgeon at the hospital. The cemetery also includes the grave of Major General William Buel Franklin. For $5.95, the York County Heritage Trust sells *A Walking Tour of Civil War-era Residents at Prospect Hill Cemetery*.

The **William Goodridge House**, 123 E. Philadelphia St., is being renovated to open as a museum of the Underground Railroad. The Goodridge mural, one of twenty murals around town, is on W. Market St., between S. Penn and Newberry Sts.

sylvania and went west, dying in Minnesota in 1873. York remembers Goodridge today with a large mural on West Market Street between South Penn and Newberry streets.

One man Goodridge helped to freedom was Osborn Perry Anderson, a black man who had participated in John Brown's raid on Harpers Ferry in 1859. Following the raid's failure and Brown's capture, Anderson managed to slip away and make his way back to Chambersburg and then on to York. With Goodridge's aid, Anderson reached Philadelphia, and then traveled to Canada, making him the only member of Brown's raiding party to escape the country.

Dennis Howard, a social worker from Springfield, Virginia, who's taking the tour this night, reveals a special interest in Anderson's story. Howard is Anderson's great-great grandson. He has been visiting places

William Goodridge, who aided escaped slaves before the Civil War, is memorialized by this mural in York.

associated with his ancestor and hopes to discover exactly how Anderson reached Canada, despite a national manhunt. "We know he got to Philadelphia," Howard says, but he hasn't determined the route from that point north.

Howard first became interested in Anderson while an eighth-grader in Alexandria, Virginia. One class assignment required the students to trace their ancestors back far enough to find a family crest. That was a reasonable requirement for white students of European descent, but something of a slap in the face for the class's only black student. "I didn't know whether to be blown away or challenged," Howard says. He decided to be challenged, and his quest has continued for forty years. His search has taken him in his great-great grandfather's footsteps through Ohio, New York, Canada, Massachusetts, and now York, Pennsylvania. By visiting a place personally, Howard says, "You can get information that is not generally known. Getting little tidbits of information from these places makes all the difference in the world."

At the tour's final stop, Butcher tells his group a story about the building at 124 East Market Street. In 1863 Judge Robert Fisher and his wife, Mary, owned this handsome brick townhouse. The judge had talked Jubal Early out of burning county records in retaliation for York's inability to raise $100,000. The story goes that when the war ended almost two years later, soldiers in York carried out a rowdy celebration. "They decided to parade through the streets of York, and of course they insisted that everyone fly the American flag," Butcher says. The Fishers didn't have a flag out, so some soldiers stopped and pounded on the door. Judge Fisher answered and said he would not submit to the demands of an unruly mob. The soldiers merely smiled and moved on—because, out of the judge's sight, his wife had quietly unfurled an American flag from an upstairs window.

The war had ended, but York's surrender left divisions that lingered for years. "There will now be a dividing line drawn here," Cassandra Small wrote in 1863 as she described Confederate sympathizers who had welcomed the Rebels to town. A. B. Farquhar felt the divisions almost as soon as Lee's army had been driven from Pennsylvania. He had traveled to Gettysburg after the battle to help the wounded there. "I had not been back in York ten minutes before I felt that something was wrong," he wrote later. "I heard jeers of 'Rebel' made at me." Farquhar's negotiations with Gordon had left him open to charges that he had sold out York to the Confederates.

The accusations troubled Farquhar so much that he went to Washington, D.C., to receive absolution from Abraham Lincoln. "You were wise not to neglect an opportunity to be of service to York and to the Union," the president told him "You go home now. And tell your fellow Yorkers that you personally have my thanks, and the thanks of the federal government for what you did in saving York from unnecessary destruction."

Hanover Junction

The invading Confederates considered railroads, which were essential for transporting troops and supplies, and telegraph wires, a vital communications link for the military, as important military targets. Hanover Junction, where the Hanover-Gettysburg and Northern Central railroads met about halfway between York and Hanover, scored on both cat-

Confederate forces targeted Hanover Junction in 1863. LIBRARY OF CONGRESS

Hanover Junction today looks much as it did when Abraham Lincoln passed through on his way to and from Gettysburg.

Hanover Junction

Hanover Junction Station's three-story red wooden station house lies on Heritage Rail Trail, which bicyclists (as well as hikers and horseback riders) can use to follow the Northern Central tracks for 21 miles from York to the Maryland state line (where Maryland's Northern Central Railroad Trail continues south for another twenty miles). The station has a small museum that's open from 10 AM to 5 PM on Saturday and 1 PM to 5 PM on Sunday, and 1 PM to 5 PM on Labor Day. The Heritage Rail Trail is open all year from 8 AM until dusk.

egories. On June 29, 1863, Lt. Col. Elijah White and his "Commanches" of the 35th Virginia Cavalry raided the railroad station and destroyed what they could. The junction had a friendlier visit on November 19, when Abraham Lincoln waited a couple hours so he could change trains here on his way to Gettysburg. Stand on the platform of the restored station today, and you can almost believe you're waiting with him. Hanover Junction Station is still visited frequently by mounted riders, but they're usually on bikes, not horses, and do little if any damage.

Susquehanna River Towns
A Bridge Too Far

Wrightsville

A pair of cannon points out across Hellam Street in Wrightsville. They sit on the crest of the rise that slopes down from this point toward the Susquehanna River. Originally dedicated in 1900, the guns mark, in the words of the plaque on their white base, "Wrightsville as the farthest point east reached by the Confederate forces, June 28, 1863."

When Brig. Gen. John B. Gordon reached this vicinity, he had a pretty good idea what to expect. Back in York, a girl had handed him a bouquet of roses. Hidden inside was a note in a woman's hand that outlined the defenses in Wrightsville, a modest town of about 1,300 people, 150 of them free blacks.

"Not an inaccurate detail in the note could be discovered," Gordon wrote in his memoirs. "There, in full view before us, was the town, just as described, nestling on the banks of the Susquehanna. There was the blue line of soldiers guarding the approach, drawn up, as indicated, along an intervening ridge and across the pike. There was the long bridge spanning the Susquehanna and connecting the town with Columbia on the other banks. Most important of all, there was the deep gorge or ravine running off to the right and extending around the left flank of the Federal line and to the river below the bridge."

By the time Gordon left Wrightsville, the blue line of Union soldiers had fled across the bridge, and the bridge itself was a smoldering ruin. Gordon's men had pushed further east than any other portion of Lee's army, but the loss of the bridge ensured they would go no further.

A pair of bridges span the Susquehanna in Wrightsville today. To the north, traffic crosses the water on U.S. Route 30. Route 462 passes right through town and across a gently curving bridge constructed in 1930. The big span, more than a mile long, runs alongside the old bridge's stone piers, which march across the river like a dotted line. They once supported a structure claimed to be the longest covered bridge in the world, a span that stretched a mile and a quarter from Wrightsville to Columbia on the opposite shore. The Confederates wanted to cross it on their way to capture Lancaster, so they could then turn around and attack Harrisburg from the rear while Maj. Gen. Robert Rodes and his division threatened it from the front.

Down by the river, the traces of the towpath for the Susquehanna and Tidewater Canal lead beneath the great sweeping arch of the 1930 bridge. When the covered bridge stood here, the canal's boatmen would drag their boats along the tow path to this point, and then across the bridge on a dual-layer towpath that allowed boats to cross in both directions, one on the top layer, the other on the bottom one.

Getting across the river was Wrightsville's reason for existence. The town got its name from John Wright, who started a ferry service across the Susquehanna in 1730. The site almost became the capital of the fledgling United States. George Washington, who occasionally crossed the river on Wright's Ferry, liked the location, but in the end the nation's capital ended up on the Potomac, not the Susquehanna. The ferry became obsolete when the first bridge across the river was completed here in 1814, three years after the town's incorporation. High water and river ice destroyed that bridge in 1832. Fire, not ice, brought down its replacement in 1863.

"The bridge was a marvel," says Don Swope. He's the president of Historic Wrightsville and today is the volunteer staff at the Burning of the Bridge Diorama, which occupies a tiny, one-room wooden building on Hellam Street. Both American and Confederate flags fly outside.

"This building originally was a post office," says Swope. "After that, it was a store for pot-bellied stoves." Photographs of Wrightsville and the bridge line the walls of the little building. Metal folding chairs surround

The burned bridge's stone piers remain in the river aside a newer bridge.

the centerpiece, a glass case, open at the top and about 5x7 feet in size, that butts up against the wall. Above it are portraits of the opposing commanders, Gen. John B. Gordon and Col. Jacob Frick.

The diorama show consists of a short recorded narration that describes the events in Wrightsville on June 28, 1863. Occasionally Swope uses a laser pointer to call attention to a specific portion of the diorama. The diorama is a neat piece of work, an example of small-town history at its finest. Little gray soldiers, some with minute muskets and others posted by tiny cannon, threaten the semi-circular Union lines that fan out around the York Turnpike as it enters town. Here and there tiny cavalry gallop on their miniscule horses, waving itsy-bitsy sabers. Little houses line the streets, and there are even tiny coal cars tipped on their sides on the approach to the bridge, just as they had been in 1863.

The model bridge itself, unfortunately, includes only four sections before it bumps into the rear of the box. What the diorama needs is a painting with forced perspective that would give a sense of just how big the bridge was, for it was indeed a marvel. It had one lane for carriages, another to accommodate the railroad, plus the dual-level towpath on the south side.

Maj. Gen. Jubal Early ordered Gordon to capture the bridge. Gordon's opponents were a ragtag bunch of about 1,400 men under Col. Jacob Frick, a thirty-six-year-old veteran of the Mexican War. His force included untested militiamen raised to face the emergency, an "Invalid Corps" of soldiers too infirm for active duty, even a company of African American volunteers, one of the first times blacks would fight in the Civil War.

Frick was sharing command, more or less, with Maj. Granville Haller, who had arrived after the townspeople in York, worried that the presence of Union soldiers would lead to Confederate destruction, asked Haller to vacate the city. Haller reached Wrightsville to find gridlock at the bridge. Hordes of panicky refugees and anything that could move on wheels, feet, or hooves waited at a bottleneck the bridge keeper had created by insisting that everyone pay the toll before crossing. Haller searched out the bridge president, who waived the tolls, and traffic began flowing smoothly.

That resolved, Frick brought his men over from Columbia. The defenders began digging some entrenchments in a horseshoe shape around the bridge's approaches, but Frick and Haller knew they couldn't hold out long against a determined foe commanding the high ground just outside town. As insurance, they had their men remove some of the

 VISITING ## Wrightsville

The **Historic Wrightsville Museum**, 309 Locust St., is housed in a circa 1897 building. It's open Sundays from 1 PM to 4 PM or by special appointment. (717) 252-1169, www.geocities.com/historicwrightsville. The museum also operates the **Burning of the Bridge Diorama**, 124 Hellam St. It is open March through November on Sundays from 1 PM to 4 PM, or by appointment.

The **John Wright Store and Restaurant**, along the water on N. Front St., claims to be "America's oldest continuously operating manufacturer of cast-iron products." The company operates from a circa-1914 brick warehouse on the banks of the Susquehanna, with great views of the bridges. The store is open Monday through Saturday 8 AM to 5 PM and Sunday 11 AM to 5 PM. The small and informal restaurant is open Monday through Saturday 8 AM to 2:45 PM and Sunday 11 AM to 2:45 PM (717) 252-2519.

bridge's supports, bore holes in the arches and fill them with gunpowder, so they could drop a section of the bridge and prevent the Confederates from crossing.

Gordon began his attack around six o'clock and soon threatened both flanks of the Union position. Sporadic artillery fire hit some buildings in town, and a cannonball decapitated one of the black volunteers in the entrenchments. Frick decided to withdraw across the bridge. Haller—perhaps his pride wounded after the Confederates had forced him first from Gettysburg and then from York—suggested that they disable the bridge *before* the Union forces could retreat across it. The men would fight harder, he said, knowing they had no other option. Frick dissuaded him from this scheme.

The defenders reached Columbia by seven thirty, and Frick gave the order to bring down the weakened span. Unfortunately, it hadn't been weakened enough, so Frick ordered the bridge set on fire. Coal oil spread on the timbers did its work well, and soon the bridge was ablaze. According to a reporter for the *York Gazette*, "The scene was magnificent. . . . . The moon was bright, and the blue clouds afforded the best contrast possible to the red glare of the conflagration. The light in the heavens must have been seen for many miles."

The Confederates tried in vain to put out the blaze. "With great energy my men labored to save the bridge," Gordon recalled. "I called on the citizens of Wrightsville for buckets and pails, but none were to be found. There was, however, no lack of buckets and pails a little later, when the town was on fire." Once the flames leapt to a nearby lumberyard and threatened Wrightsville, Confederates and townspeople became allies and formed a bucket brigade from the river to the town. One house they saved was that of the town's burgess, James Magee.

To thank the enemy soldiers for saving the house, Magee's daughter, Mrs. Luther L. Rewalt, invited Gordon and as many of his men as she could accommodate to the house for breakfast the next morning. There, Gordon discreetly hinted that perhaps she might have some Southern sympathies. She set him straight. "I am a Union woman," she said. "You and your soldiers last night saved my home from burning, and I was unwilling that you should go away without receiving some token of my appreciation. I must tell you, however, that, with my assent and approval, my husband is a soldier in the Union army, and my constant prayer to Heaven is that our cause may triumph and the Union be saved."

Gordon described Mrs. Rewalt as "one of the most superb women it was my fortune to meet during the four years of war." Sometimes it was a civil war.

The house where Gordon breakfasted stands today on Hellam Street, a narrow brick building on the banking that rises above the sidewalk. Adorning the small, high front porch is a handmade wooden sign that says "Support Our Troops." Mrs. Rewalt—who happens to be novelist Gore Vidal's grandmother—would have appreciated the sentiment.

The bridge was destroyed, but Swope points out a chunk of wood that rests against one wall in the diorama building. According to legend, this is a piece of the burned bridge. "There were lots of big pieces floating down the Susquehanna," says Swope, "and a piece went ashore on the Lancaster side and became part of a barn." When the barn was torn down sometime around the early 1930s, a local man retrieved the timber and later passed it on to a collector.

Swope also points out a photograph of the Locust Street United Methodist Church, which supposedly still bears some scars from the Confederate shelling. "I can't see it," he says with a laugh, "but they say it's there."

Columbia

Columbia is a compact riverside town that seems to be made entirely of brick. It boasts a number of handsome Victorian houses, and it's a place where you can still step back to the '60s—although it's the 1960s, nicely encapsulated in Hinkle's Pharmacy, where you can sit in a booth and order a reasonably priced meal topped off with apple pie and ice cream.

Hinkle's is a relative newcomer to Columbia. The town dates back to 1726, when it became known as the "Gateway to the West." In the years before the Civil War, it gained a reputation as an important "station" along the Underground Railroad, the informal and surreptitious routes escaped slaves took to find freedom in the North. The name Underground Railroad may have derived from an incident in Columbia when slave hunters, angry and frustrated by their inability to find any fugitives, said, "There must be an underground railroad somewhere."

The Underground Railroad provides some of the stories that Terri Darden tells on her African American heritage tours of the Columbia area. Darden, a poet and playwright from Lancaster, began offering her tours after she began her own quest to discover her history. "I found

Columbia

A good place to begin exploring the area is at the **Susquehanna Valley Chamber of Commerce and Visitor Center**, at 445 Linden St. at the intersection with Fifth St. The center offers the full range of brochures and booklets from area attractions. (717) 684-5249, www.parivertowns.com.

Further down Fifth St., below the Route 30 overpass, you'll find **Zion Hill Cemetery**, the final resting place of African American veterans of the Civil War, including men who fought the Confederates at Wrightsville. Shadowed by tall trees, this small cemetery is very pretty but none-too-quiet because of the constant rush of traffic from Route 30.

For a retro experience of another time—the 1960s instead of the 1860s—stop by **Hinkle's Pharmacy**, Third and Locust Sts. It has been in business since 1893 and still provides a good place to stop for a quick meal—in a booth or at the counter—or a root beer float. (717) 684-2552.

Columbia has several large antique centers. **The Burning Bridge Antiques Market**, 304 Walnut St., opened in 2005 in a brick building that dates to around 1880. Hours are Monday through Wednesday 10 AM to 5 PM, Thursday and Friday 10 AM to 8 PM, Saturday from 10 AM to 5 PM, and Sunday from noon to 5 PM. (717) 684-7900. The **Columbia Rivertowne Antique Center**, near the waterfront at 125 Bank Ave., is in an 1872 tobacco warehouse. It's open daily except Tuesdays from 10 AM to 5 PM. (717) 684-8514,

there were slaves in Pennsylvania," she says. "I thought it was a free state. So I started researching and I found that there were 4,000 slaves in Lancaster County." She set out to gather the names of every one of them, gathered from libraries, church records, historical societies, genealogists, and historians.

Initially, Darden wanted to establish a monument to the county's slaves, until people at Lancaster's downtown investment district suggested she start her own nonprofit organization to explore African American history. Eventually she did just that. On January 19, 2005, Darden offered her first tour through Tribute at Freedom's Crossing, Inc.

On her Columbia tour, which features living historians at a number of stops, Darden tells the story of Stephen Smith, a successful African

www.rivertowneantiques.com. **Partners & Friends Antique Center**, 403 No. 3rd St., is open Monday through Saturday, 10 AM to 5 PM, and Sunday noon to 5 PM. (717) 684-5364.

If you have the time, stop by the **National Watch & Clock Museum**, 514 Poplar St. Clockwatchers will find the largest collection of timepieces on the continent, from throughout the ages and around the world. (717) 684-8261, www.nawcc.org. It's open Tuesday through Saturday, 10 AM to 5 PM, and Sunday noon to 4 PM (reduced hours in winter). There is an admission charge.

Wright's Ferry Mansion, 38 S. Second St., was built in 1738 by Susanna Wright. The long and narrow limestone building is open from May to October on Tuesday, Wednesday, Friday, and Saturday from 10 AM to 3 PM. There is an admission charge. The **Columbia Museum of History**, 19–21 Second St., is open Sundays from 1:30 PM to 4:30 PM. They request a donation. The **First National Bank Museum**, 170 Locust St., is undergoing restoration but is open for tours by appointment. The bank dates to the 1850s and still includes original furnishings and equipment. (717) 684-8864, www.bankmuseum.org. There is a fee.

Tribute at Freedom's Crossing, Inc., offers a number of African American–themed tours of the Columbia-Wrightsville area. Among them is a three-hour tour of local Underground Railroad history. Cost is $25 for adults and $18 for students. There are regularly scheduled tours, but groups interested in other dates can call and inquire about availability. (717) 252-0229, www.padutchcountry.com/columbiatour.

American businessman. His success aroused the ire of whites who resented having to compete against a black man. The friction sparked race riots in 1834 and 1835. The tours visit the museum at the First National Bank, in which Smith was a major stock holder. She also visits two cemeteries, Zion Hill and Mt. Bethel, to see the final resting places of African American soldiers from the Civil War, including veterans of the 54th and 55th Massachusetts regiments.

Back in 1995, Darden decided on the name Freedom's Crossing for her future business. Ten years later, she learned that runaway slaves used the same name for the spot on the river beneath the Wrightsville Bridge, where they could look across the wide Susquehanna toward Columbia. Darden thought her choice of name must have been destiny.

VISITING   # Marietta

Marietta, just a few miles north of Columbia on the Susquehanna River, is a charming town with many historic buildings. In fact, almost half the town is listed on the National Register of Historic Places. **The Restoration Associates' Old Town Hall Museum**, Waterford St., is in a building that dates from 1847. The museum is open Saturday 10 AM to 3 PM and Sunday from 1 PM to 3 PM, or by appointment. (717) 426-4317. Across the street is **Union Hall**, built in 1818. The **Railroad House** restaurant and bed and breakfast, 280 W. Front St., is a sturdy, brick structure facing the railroad that runs alongside the Susquehanna. It has eight rooms inside, plus the Summer Kitchen guest room off the patio. Thomas Scott, a Pennsylvanian railroad magnate who served under Simon Cameron as assistant secretary of war and helped prepare Harrisburg's defenses, owned the house in the 1890s. (717) 426-4141, www.therailroadhouse.com.

Hanover
Fighting in the Streets

Hanover doesn't look like a Civil War battlefield. Yes, a pair of cannon sit on the edge of the main square, and a statue of a mounted cavalryman keeps watch on the opposite corner, but other than that, Hanover looks like a typical Pennsylvania town.

On June 30, 1863, Hanover was anything but typical, as Northern and Southern cavalries fought a running battle through its streets.

On the evening of the battle's 143rd anniversary, licensed Gettysburg guide Larry Wallace prepares to take a group out on a walking tour of Hanover. The tour starts at the Neas House, a handsome Georgian mansion on Chestnut Street that was built in 1783 by Mathias Neas and today serves as a museum for the Hanover Area Historical Society.

The biggest names in Civil War cavalry clashed here at Hanover in 1863. Jeb Stuart represented the Confederacy, while George Armstrong Custer and Judson Kilpatrick were here for the Union. But Wallace says, "This was not a classic cavalry battle." The fight that took place on East Cavalry Field at Gettysburg four days later, in which mounted horsemen battled each other, was. "This was different, because it was urban warfare," Wallace says. "You were confined to the streets or the alleys." The combatants would not have chosen to fight in the town, Wallace adds, but in this case that's where the enemy was.

Rumors of war had been unnerving the citizens of Hanover, a small town of about 1,600, for some time. "Our town has been in an intense state of excitement during the last few days," said the *Hanover Spectator*

Relics of the Civil War on the square in Hanover.

in an editorial on June 19, 1863. "A thousand and one rumors are circulated in the course of the day of such a conflicting character that it is impossible to give a correct statement of the actual condition of affairs."

Rumors crystallized into fact on June 27, when Confederate cavalry under Elijah White rode into town. These men of the 35th Virginia were known as the Commanches, and they had a reputation for wild behavior. Two arrived in advance of the rest, who followed in a column four abreast down Carlisle Street to the town square. They rode cautiously, fingers on their triggers, as frightened townspeople peeped out from behind their shutters. A group of men gathered in front of the Central Hotel, and White stopped to give a short speech, remarking that despite their shabby appearance, his men would not harm anyone. They did, however, dismount and purchase some supplies from Hanover stores, paying with useless Confederate money. One Virginian strode into the A. G. Schmidt drugstore and demanded a bottle of whiskey. The Commanches then rode out of town to burn bridges and tear down telegraph lines on their way to join Gen. John Gordon for his march to Wrightsville.

Hanover, now cut off from the outside world, waited in fearful anticipation of what would happen next. Telegraph operator Daniel Trone, whose house still stands at 233 Frederick Street, knew he'd be a target, so he hid his equipment in a loft and left two broken sets on a table in his office as decoys before fleeing. "We received no newspapers; the telegraph wires were cut, and all we could learn of the movement of the Union or Confederate forces toward Gettysburg was gathered from rumors," remembered the Reverend K. Zieber, the pastor at the Emmanuel Reformed Church and the head of Hanover's Committee of Safety.

Jeb Stuart reached town by a roundabout route. Following a surprise attack by Union cavalry at Brandy Station, Virginia, Stuart dueled with Federal horsemen in the Shenandoah Valley as his men blocked passes and prevented the Yankees from discerning Lee's movements. On June 22, Stuart received orders from Lee to protect the army's right flank, harass the enemy, gather supplies, and provide intelligence about Union troop movements. Early in the morning on June 25, Stuart set out, but the presence of Federal forces forced him to make a wide detour. On the night of the 27th, Stuart's men made a daring crossing of the Potomac into Maryland, despite deep, fast-flowing water that submerged the artillery and almost swept the men from their horses. "No more difficult achievement was accomplished by the cavalry during the war," wrote H. B. McClellan, one of Stuart's officers (and cousin to the Union's General McClellan).

In Rockville, Maryland, Stuart's men captured 125 Union wagons on their way to supply the Army of the Potomac. It must have seemed an ideal opportunity to gather supplies for Lee, as Stuart's orders specified.

Stuart's men continued their way north and into Pennsylvania, skirmishing with local militia, burning bridges, and destroying railroad track and telegraph lines. They cut off direct communication between General Meade and Washington, D.C., which meant messages between the general and the capital had to travel via Harrisburg. At around ten o'clock on the morning on June 30, Stuart's men reached the outskirts of Hanover.

Maj. Gen. Judson Kilpatrick and his cavalry were already there, having reached town about two hours earlier. Kilpatrick, twenty-six, had just received command of the Union cavalry's 3rd Division. He had a prominent nose and bushy sideburns that gave him the appearance of a debauched leprechaun, and his soldiers nicknamed him "Kill Cavalry," and not necessarily out of respect. Kilpatrick sought glory and he snatched at it any way he could, even if it meant his men died for it.

Kilpatrick wasn't the only glory seeker in Hanover. One of his subordinates was George Armstrong Custer, whose promotion to brigadier

The men who served under Maj. Gen. Judson Kilpatrick called him "Kill Cavalry."
LIBRARY OF CONGRESS

general the day before made him, at age twenty-three, the Union's youngest general. He had graduated last in his class at West Point, only three days before fighting at First Manassas, and like Kilpatrick he had an unquenching thirst for glory. Some said he was reckless, but no one doubted his courage, or his talent for attracting attention. When Custer reached Hanover, he was wearing a uniform of black velvet with gold-lace trim, a shirt with wide collars bearing silver stars, a bright red tie, and a rakishly tilted black hat with a golden cord. It was, another officer noted, "a unique outfit."

In Hanover, Kilpatrick and Custer stopped at the house of Jacob Wirt and told a gathering of citizens that their men were hungry. The Reverend Zieber spread word around town, and residents began arriving with food and drink. Kilpatrick and Custer, meanwhile, headed north toward Abbotstown, while members of Brig. Gen. Elon Farnsworth's division remained in Hanover. Further south, the 18th Pennsylvania Cavalry rested around the house and farm owned by Karl Forney. It was a new regiment, untested in battle. The test came suddenly, when the 13th Virginia and 2nd North Carolina Cavalry attacked the Union horsemen and pushed them north down Frederick Street, toward the center of Hanover.

Further north, Maj. John Hammond and the 5th New York Cavalry were enjoying Hanover's hospitality. The peaceful interlude ended when an artillery shell burst overhead. Hammond began urging the civilians to seek shelter in their basements. "In a few minutes there will be fighting in your streets," he warned. Members of the 18th Pennsylva-

George A. Custer arrived in Hanover as a newly promoted brigadier general.
LIBRARY OF CONGRESS

Hanover

The **Hanover Area Chamber of Commerce**, 146 Carlisle St., publishes a brochure that outlines a Battle of Hanover Walking Tour. (717) 637-6130, www.hanoverchamber.com.

The **Hanover Area Historical Society**, 105 High St., has office hours Monday, Wednesday, and Friday from 9 AM to 2 PM. (717) 632-3207, www.hanoverareahistoricalsociety.org. The Society operates the **Neas House Museum**, 113 W. Chestnut St. Built in 1783, the Georgian brick building was home to George Neas, Hanover's first burgess. It's open during the historical society's office hours. There is an admission charge.

The **German Reformed Cemetery**, 116 York St., is behind the Trinity United Church of Christ. (717) 637-2233, www.trinityucchanover.org.

People who read religiously will want to visit **The Readers' Café**, 125 Broadway, a little bookstore that makes its home in a former Presbyterian church. If you're not tipped off by its outside appearance, you will be when you step inside and gaze up at the old wooden beams of its arched roof. (717) 630-2524.

Established in 1980, the **Hanover Fire Museum**, 201 N. Franklin St., includes an 1882 Silsby Steamer, an 1830 hand pumper, and a 1770 hand engine, as well as other fire fighting memorabilia. The museum is in the current fire station and is staffed by members of the fire fighting department. It's open daily from 10 AM to 8 PM. (717) 637-6671, www.borough.hanover.pa.us/images/hanover/hbfiremuseum.html.

Many Hanover residents from the time of the battle are buried at **Mount Olivet Cemetery**, 725 Baltimore St. Telegraph operator Daniel Trone is here, and so is newspaperwoman Mary Shaw Leader, who walked to Gettysburg to hear Lincoln speak. The Soldiers' Memorial includes the names of the area's Civil War soldiers. (717) 637-5294.

nia began rushing past, pursued by the attacking Confederates. Soon the entire Union contingent was retreating down Frederick Street toward the town Diamond.

Hammond and the bedraggled Union horsemen reformed their lines on Abbotstown Street (now Broadway) north of the square at the

Public Commons and prepared a counterattack. With drawn sabers, the Union cavalry charged back toward the square and reversed the Confederate tide. Now the Union advanced south, and the Confederates retreated before them.

Ambrose M. Schmidt was a boy in Hanover at the time. "My mother was on our porch with us children when a Union officer came and sat down with us," he recalled years later. "Suddenly, a shell exploded in the direction of Frederick Street. He at once leaped to his feet, ran to his horse, and exclaimed, 'My God, woman, the Confederates are upon us! Get your children into the house.' He then dashed out Abbotstown Street. We could not have been there more than a few moments when the cavalry forces met on Broadway, right before us. We ran into the house, crying."

Schmidt and his family took refuge in the basement of their hardware store on the square, entering through a wooden door set flat at sidewalk level. Throughout the battle they listened, terrified, as horses hoofs galloped across the wooden door. "I recall how fearful my parents were, lest that cellar door should prove too weak to bear the weight of the horses," recalled Schmidt.

The reverse came so suddenly that the Union troops threatened to reach Stuart, who had been observing the battle from a field south of the Forney Farm. Stuart wheeled his horse around and leapt across a ditch that contained a small stream. "Splendidly mounted on his favorite mare Virginia, Stuart took the ditch at a running leap, and landed safely on the other side, with several feet to spare," recounted H. B. McClellan. "Some of his party made the leap with equal success, but not a few horses failed, and landed their riders in shallow water, whence by energetic scrambling they reached the safe side of the stream. The ludicrousness of the situation, notwithstanding the peril, was the source of much merriment at the expense of these unfortunate ones."

The creek—if the sign is in the right places—is long gone on this sun-baked portion of Frederick Street now, although there is a small creek to the south, where Hanover peters out and Pennsylvania's rolling farmland resumes.

It was at a spot near here that Lt. Col. W. H. Payne of the 4th Virginia Cavalry, who was in temporary command of the 2nd North Carolina, fell into enemy hands. His horse had been shot out from under him, and threw Payne into a tanning vat at the Winebrenner tannery. His captors hauled him out, stained and dripping, and sent him to the Central Hotel to be questioned by Kilpatrick and Custer.

The sound of guns had brought those two officers charging back into town. Kilpatrick had reached Abbotstown before he turned around. He returned to Hanover in record time, but at the expense of his horse, which died from its exertions. Kilpatrick made his headquarters in Room 24 of the Central Hotel on the square.

Custer also retraced his steps back to Hanover, where he tied his horse to a silver maple opposite the Central Hotel. Resident J. W. Gitt had planted the tree in 1850. Years later, when the city wanted to remove the decaying "Custer Maple," Gitt sued to keep it. He won a case that went all the way to the Pennsylvania Supreme Court. The tree was finally taken down in 1924, but a tablet on the side of the M&T Bank building tells its story and commemorates both "the gallant soldier who fought here" and "the citizen who fought to preserve that soldier's original monument—'the Custer Maple.'" A bronze star surrounded by four bronze horseshoes embedded in the sidewalk marks the spot where the tree grew.

It's right next to the two Union cannon, 2.9-inch Parrott rifles that aim across the square at the statue of the Union cavalryman. The statue, called *The Pickett*, represents all the Union cavalry who fought here. It's the work of Boston sculptor Cyrus E. Dallin and was unveiled in 1905 at a ceremony that included men who had fought the Confederates here forty-two years earlier. The statue and the cannon had originally stood in the center of the square, until the demands of modern traffic forced their relocation.

After the Union horsemen forced the Rebels from the square, the combatants settled into a tense standoff. The Confederates set up artillery south of town, and the Union put their batteries on Bunker Hill to the north. At the Winebrenner House down Frederick Street, a Confederate artillery shell crashed through the door on the second-floor balcony, passed through a bureau, and continued through the floor, coming out in the first-floor sitting room where the whole family had taken shelter. Fortunately, the shell did not explode, and Mr. Winebrenner tossed it outside. The house is a private residence today, in a shady block of handsome brick and clapboard buildings. The door with the shell hole is still in the house, while the shell is part of the collections of the Hanover Area Historical Society.

The Pickett in Hanover honors the Union cavalry that clashed with Stuart's brigades there.

After some inconclusive skirmishing, Kilpatrick left a small force at Hanover and moved north. Stuart and the Confederates moved off to the southeast and then resumed their search for Jubal Early, whom Stuart hoped to join at York. Because of the delay at Hanover, Stuart missed crossing paths with Old Jube, who had already left York on his way to Gettysburg. Stuart continued north through Dillsburg and then turned toward Carlisle. By then, Lee and Meade's armies had already stumbled together at Gettysburg, and Stuart didn't reach the battle until its second day. The delay at Hanover had cost the Confederates dearly, depriving Lee of Stuart's eyes and ears during the battle's opening.

But Larry Wallace warns his tour group of attaching *too* much importance to the battle in Hanover's streets. "What happened here was a factor in Lee's defeat," he says, "but saying the battle of Hanover is why Lee lost at Gettysburg is an oversimplification in the greatest degree. It's one of the reasons Lee lost, but it's not the only reason, obviously."

Telegraph operator Daniel Trone returned to Hanover after the battle was over. Rebel cavalrymen had smashed the decoy telegraph equipment, but they did not find the good set in the loft. Trone retrieved his hidden equipment, and for the next two days telegraphed information

Some of the dead from the battle of Hanover are buried by the Civil War memorial in Mount Olivet Cemetery.

about the Gettysburg battle in an exclusive arrangement with the *New York Tribune*. Abraham Lincoln received his first news of the battle from reports that Trone sent to New York through Washington.

The Battle of Hanover had been small by Civil War standards, certainly compared to what started a day later at Gettysburg. The Union suffered some 215 causalities, dead and wounded, while the Confederate casualties numbered 117. For the citizens of Hanover, this taste of war was more than enough. Doctors treated the wounded right where they found them. The Reverend Zieber pulled dead men from the streets. Some of the Union dead were buried in the town's German Reformed Cemetery, but they were later exhumed and reinterred at the new National Cemetery in Gettysburg. The man in charge of the reinterrments was Samuel Weaver; his son, Peter, was a photographer with a shop on Baltimore Street in Hanover. He took some photographs of the grisly business of exhumation.

One reporter who covered Lincoln's speech at the National Cemetery's dedication was Mary Shaw Leader, who walked all the way from Hanover to write about the event for her family's paper, the *Hanover Spectator*. She called the Gettysburg Address "a remarkable speech." Leader's grave, with a new stone installed in 1941, is in Hanover's Mount Olivet Cemetery.

Abraham Lincoln's train stopped briefly in Hanover on its way to Gettysburg, and the brief visit prompted George W. Gitt, son of the Custer Maple's J. W. Gitt, to make the trip to Gettysburg to hear the president speak. He crawled beneath the speaker's platform and listened to the Gettysburg Address while lying on his back and gazing up at Lincoln's feet through the spaces between the boards. Afterwards young Gitt shook hands with the president at the Wills house in town, and then started back home to Hanover, a town that had also become a battlefield.

Gettysburg
High-Water Mark

Cars pull into the traffic circle by the Virginia Memorial at Gettysburg National Military Park and stop beneath the unblinking gaze of the Robert E. Lee statue high above. Confederate soldiers and women in large crinoline skirts climb out from the vehicles. The women shade themselves with parasols as the men remove flags from the trunks and buckle on sword belts. It is July 3, and these twenty-first-century Rebels are members of the Civil War Heritage Foundation, here to recreate Pickett's Charge on its 143rd anniversary.

Pickett himself is portrayed by Paul Karabin, the owner of Pickett's General Store in Perth, New York. He looks uncomfortably hot in his uniform as he prepares to walk across the fields to the "high-water mark of the Confederacy." "If you see a horse, send him my way," Karabin says. His wife, awaiting him on the battlefield's opposite side, often portrays Pickett's wife, Sallie, and Karabin says the couple just renewed their vows in the presence of a General Lee impersonator.

Karabin pulls on his white gauntlets as the small group of reenactors mills about their staging area. Things are somewhat different than they were in 1863. The Confederates today number maybe twenty-five, a little short of the 15,000 that advanced from the woods here on the battle's third day, in a last-ditch effort to dislodge the Union forces from Cemetery Ridge opposite. And park regulations prohibit these Rebels from carrying firearms or even drawing their swords.

Beneath the relentless sun, the small band of sweltering Confederates receive their final briefing. "When we get to the top, we'll receive a

Civil War reenactors arrive in Gettysburg every year in July to recreate the battle for visitors.

A statue of Robert E. Lee on his mount Traveler sits on the crest of the Virginia Memorial in Gettysburg.

very different welcome than the boys received back then," their colonel tells them. He slaps his sword. "We don't have to worry about running into these." Then, at three o'clock, the Rebels step off and begin their march across the wide field. Soon only their banners are visible off in the distance.

Lee's Pennsylvania campaign reached its peak here, the climax of a bloody three-day battle that marked a turning point in the war. A small grove of trees on the opposite side of the field marks the most distant point the attackers reached before being driven back. The copse of trees is called "the high-water mark of the Confederacy." The Civil War dragged on for almost two more years, but Gettysburg—and the Union victory at Vicksburg in Mississippi at the same time—marked the beginning of the end for the South.

Each year, two million people visit Gettysburg to see the battlefield. They also dine at Pickett's Charge Buffet, at O'Rorke's, a restaurant named after the Union colonel who fell leading his men to blunt the Confederates at Little Round Top, or at the Farnsworth House Inn, a period building that still bears bullet holes. It's named after Brig. Gen. Elon John Farnsworth, who died on July 3 during a typically rash cavalry charge ordered by Judson Kilpatrick. Diners there today gaze upon a selection of relics from the movie *Gettysburg,* in a strange melding of the real and the imitation. Visitors can buy souvenirs at the Irish Brigade Gift Shop or any of the several stores that sell everything from Joshua Chamberlain T-shirts to an authentic cavalry major's coat, which will set you back $16,500 at the Union Drummer Boy on Baltimore Street. On the sidewalks, myriad ghost tours battle each other for customers who want a good scare. War is hell, as William Tecumseh Sherman almost said, but it's also good for business.

Some of Gettysburg's businesses date from a time when tourists were still impressed by dioramas, wax figures, and grainy films. These attractions are the stuff of field trips past, when summer vacation meant a long drive in a hot station wagon to climb on a cannon, buy a wooden gun, and perhaps learn a little history. The current visitor center also belongs to a different age. The building dates from the 1920s and is small, crowded, and somewhat shabby. Inside, it has displays of guns, swords, uniforms, and cannon. Some spaces are also filled with the roar of the air-conditioning units that labor mightily to maintain the right temperature and humidity for the collections.

The showcase attraction is the Electric Map, which sits in the middle of a little amphitheater of hard wooden chairs with folding seats. Once the show begins, blue and orange lights blink on and off, accompanied by the sound of clicking switches, to illustrate the movement of Union and Confederate troops. The map is undeniably old-fashioned, but there's something comforting about its unintentional nostalgia.

However, there are changes afoot for Gettysburg. A brand-new visitors center with state-of-the-art displays and artifact storage is scheduled to open off Baltimore Pike in the spring of 2008. The current visitor center and the circular Cyclorama Building, which housed a gigantic circular painting of the battle, will be torn down so this portion of Cemetery Ridge can be restored to its 1863 appearance. The restored Cyclorama will have a home in the new visitor center.

Other portions of the battlefield are changing too. The park service has been restoring the terrain so it once again resembles the ground the Civil War combatants knew. In some places trees have been cut down. In others, notably the Peach Orchard, new trees will be planted. One thing Gettysburg won't see anytime soon is a casino. A battle had been raging ever since Crossroads Gaming Resort and Spa selected a site in the area for a proposed gambling establishment. Opponents decried the idea of a casino so near the battlefield's hallowed ground, while proponents touted the economic benefits. In December 2006, the opponents won the battle when the state's Gaming Control Board eliminated Adams County as a casino location.

Another thing that won't change is the profusion of statues and memorials—some 1,400 of them, plus 400 cannon—that make portions of the battlefield's twenty-five square miles feel like a gigantic sculpture garden. Most of the memorials commemorate the individual regiments that fought here, and were placed by their survivors. These memorials come in all shapes and sizes. Some depict soldiers—sitting, standing, lying down, shooting, stabbing, running into battle. The 42nd New York Infantry's memorial is a large bronze of an American Indian, Chief Tammaned, standing in front of a very detailed tepee. The 42nd was known as the Tammany Regiment, after the political organization that helped raise it.

Union and Confederate armies fought here for three long days, and a visitor can easily spend that much time getting a good sense of the battlefield. The National Park Service has mapped out a couple of driving tours, which provide a good overview of the battle. Bicycles and horses

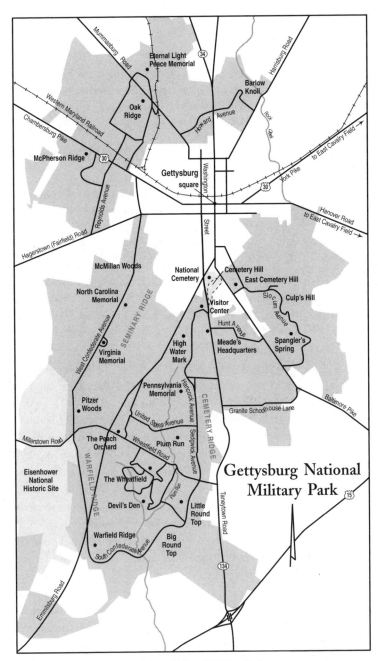

Gettysburg National Military Park

provide alternate methods of exploring. Licensed guides are available at the visitor center to give a more personalized look at things.

Back in 1988, Wayne Motts became one of the National Park Service's youngest battlefield guides as a mere stripling of twenty-one. Even then he had some experience. Motts gave his first lecture about Gettysburg and the Civil War to students in a master's program at Ohio State when he was only fourteen. Today Motts is executive director of the Adams County Historical Society, and he keeps a copy of a local newspaper account about the lecture on the wall above his desk. "Whiz Kid," reads the headline.

Motts, rail thin with glasses and slicked-back hair, says his father was "a huge Civil War buff," so family vacations often meant a trip from the Motts home in Ohio to Gettysburg, sometimes five times a year. "All my life I've been interested in the Civil War," he says. His interest was sparked by diaries that had been given to his father, written by a white Union soldier who died during the attack on Fort Wagner in South Carolina, a battle depicted in the movie *Glory*. "My father used to open them when I was a little boy and read excerpts, including when this man met Lincoln," Motts says. "So for me, one of the things that got me interested was this personal connection."

Now Motts works inside the Lutheran Seminary's old main building, a place with its own personal connections to the battle and the men who fought and died here. When Brig. Gen. John Buford of the Union's 1st Cavalry division reached Gettysburg on June 30, he climbed up into the cupola here to survey the approaching Confederates. During and after the battle, the building served as a hospital, the floors slick with blood, and the grounds outside piled with amputated limbs. Motts estimates that some 600 wounded men were treated in the building, including Confederate generals James Kemper and Isaac Trimble, both wounded during Pickett's Charge. At least sixty Union soldiers died in the building, and historians have identified eighty patients by name. The staff of the historical society recently found images of fourteen men who were treated here, another personal connection with the events from 1863.

Those fourteen were just a tiny fraction of Gettysburg's 51,000 causalities. The battle here was a bloodbath of the worst kind, leaving the fields, hills, and woods littered with the corpses of soldiers and horses. Gettysburg businesses today may give thanks for the millions of people who visit each year to walk the killing fields, but in 1863 the town's residents wished that the Union and Confederate armies had collided somewhere else.

In fact, they almost did. Neither Lee nor Meade had planned to fight here. The newly promoted commander of the Army of the Potomac wanted to meet Lee's army just over the state line in Maryland, on a fine defensive position along the banks of Pipe Creek south of Taneytown. Events overtook both generals, however, and the armies met in Pennsylvania, not Maryland.

"It is remarkable that, in the one Pennsylvania battle of the war, the men of that State should have borne so prominent a part," noted one Union general. "It was a Pennsylvanian [Meade] who directed the movement on Gettysburg and commanded there in chief. It was a Pennsylvanian [Reynolds] who hurried the left wing into action and lost his life in determining that the battle should be fought at Gettysburg, and not at any line more remote. It was a Pennsylvanian [Hancock] who came up to check the rout and hold Cemetery Hill for the Union arms, who commanded the left center in the great battle of the second day, and on the third received and repelled the attack of Pettigrew and Pickett."

The battle began by accident on July 1, when Henry Heth's Confederate division, from A. P. Hill's III Corps, marched down the Chambersburg Pike and encountered resistance north of Gettysburg along Willoughby Run. Legend has it that Heth's soldiers were heading to Gettysburg to get shoes. Whatever the truth—it doesn't appear that shoes had anything to do with it—Lee had ordered his generals to avoid a full engagement, and Heth disregarded those orders. He later said he thought his men had simply encountered local militia. Heth pushed forward, but these Union troops pushed back.

Heth had run into the Union 1st Cavalry under Buford, a tougher-than-leather professional soldier who quickly assessed the situation, sent a message back to Maj. Gen. John Reynolds, commander of Meade's I Corps, and prepared to give the Confederates a warm welcome to Gettysburg. Buford's statue stands today by the side of U.S. Route 30,

Pennsylvania native Maj. Gen. John Reynolds died on the first day of the battle at Gettysburg. MILITARY HISTORY INSTITUTE

peering westward down the Chambersburg Pike with field glasses in hand. Set in concrete blocks around the pedestal are four Union cannon, one of them supposedly the gun that fired the first artillery shot of the Gettysburg battle. (A small marker further west on U.S. Route 30 credits Lt. Marcellus Ephraim Jones of the 8th Illinois Cavalry with firing the very first shot, from a borrowed carbine.)

Reynolds's statue stands behind Buford's. Reynolds is mounted, and two of his horse's hoofs are lifted, an unofficial code indicating the rider died in battle. (This code was broken in 1998 with the statue of James Longstreet.) Reynolds, considered one of the Union's best soldiers, reached the battlefield with his men just in time, as Buford's dismounted troopers were about to break beneath the weight of the Confederate advance. He had hardly begun to position his soldiers when a Confederate bullet struck him in the head and killed him. A spare stone monument off Reynolds Avenue marks the spot where he tumbled to the ground, dead.

Gettysburg resident John Burns had served during the War of 1812 and was determined to fight for his country when Confederates reached his town. LIBRARY OF CONGRESS

One of Reynolds's most dependable units was the Iron Brigade, which took positions in the woods behind Willoughby Run. The men with their trademark black hats proceeded to make things difficult for the advancing Confederates. They had a little extra help, too, from a cantankerous sixty-nine-year-old Gettysburg resident named John Burns. His statue stands on Stone Avenue, musket in one hand (though he actually used a rifle), and the other hand clenched in grim determination.

Burns was a veteran of the War of 1812 and wanted to fight for his country. "It must have been about noon when I saw a little old man coming up in the rear of Company F," remembered a sergeant in the 7th Wisconsin. "In regard to the peculiarities of his dress, I remember he wore a swallow-tailed coat with smooth brass buttons. He had a rifle on his shoulder. We boys began to poke fun as soon as he came amongst us, as we thought no civilian in his senses would show himself in such a place." As bullets flew and the soldiers hit the dirt, Burns stood behind a tree and returned the fire, "as calm and collected as any veteran on the ground." Burns survived the battle with three wounds, and was lionized as "the old hero of Gettysburg."

For a time, the Union line held, but then men from Richard Ewell's II Corps began arriving from the northwest, and the Federals—especially Maj. Gen. Oliver O. Howard's XI Corps—crumbled. The Union soldiers began to retreat, back through the town of Gettysburg toward the defensible heights of Cemetery Hill.

Suddenly, Gettysburg itself was a battlefield. The casual park visitor might miss this aspect of the fighting, but the town recognizes it with a number of streetside markers throughout the borough that tell fascinating stories of ordinary people swept up in extraordinary events. "After all these years, it's amazing how many still come to this town, thinking all the fighting took place in the park that surrounds it," says Nancie Gudmestad, director of the Shriver House Museum on Baltimore Street.

At the time, Gettysburg had a population of 2,400. It was a busy crossroads where ten roads met, and it had been the county seat since 1800. Two institutions of higher learning, Pennsylvania (now Gettysburg) College and the Lutheran Seminary, called Gettysburg home. It did not seem like the kind of place to fight a battle.

Time has marched on since then, but Baltimore Street, a wide, handsome avenue that runs from the town's central square—its Diamond—toward Cemetery Hill, retains some nineteenth-century char-

Tillie Pierce, fifteen, fled south from her home on Baltimore Street, only to find herself in the thick of things near Little Round Top. ADAMS COUNTY HISTORICAL SOCIETY

acter. Many of the buildings that stand here witnessed the battle, and some of them still bear scars from the fighting.

The Shrivers lived at number 309, now the Shriver House Museum. In 1863 this handsome brick house was only three years old. George Shriver (sometimes spelled Schriver) was preparing to open a saloon in the basement and a Tenpin Alley—a bowling alley—out back. Before he had a chance to launch this new business, war broke out and George joined a Union cavalry regiment. He was later captured and sent to Andersonville Prison, where he died.

His wife Hettie and daughters Sadie, five, and Mollie, seven, remained behind in Gettysburg, and the war came to them, announced by the roaring of guns outside town. On July 1, Hettie took her daughters and Tillie Pierce, a pretty fifteen-year-old who lived next door, and headed south to the farm of Hettie's father, Jacob Weikert. The farmhouse, a small stone building with a columned porch, stood on the backside of a hill called Little Round Top. Hettie did not realize, of course, that she was simply moving from the frying pan into the fire.

While Hettie was gone, Confederate sharpshooters occupied the house. They knocked out bricks from the south wall of the garret, and fired through these improvised loopholes at the Union soldiers on Cemetery Hill. Tillie Pierce's father, peering through his garret window next door, saw one of the sharpshooters hit by a Union bullet and die.

Nancie Gudmestad and her husband bought the house in 1996, and they decided to restore it to its 1863 appearance and open it as a museum. During the restoration, a brick mason removed patches from the garret's outside wall and found the loopholes. The garret revealed other surprises. "We did have to pull up some floorboards to do some work underneath, and that was really the luckiest thing that happened," Gudmestad says. Beneath them, they found six Civil War bullets, three of them still with their paper cartridges and gunpowder intact. Civil War medical equipment had been hidden away under other boards. The bullets and medical supplies are now on display in the museum, along with other artifacts lost in the walls and beneath the floors over the years—everything from a 1966 *Mad* magazine to a Herbert Hoover campaign brochure.

Even more amazingly, a crime scene investigator from New York recently visited the house to test a reagent used to detect blood stains. He wanted to see if the chemical would work with very old samples. When the detective smeared the substance on the floor in front of the loopholes, Gudmestad says, "It glowed like there was no tomorrow. And all around the portholes there was blood splattered all over the place." They could even see swipe marks that someone—perhaps Hettie— made trying to clean up the blood. "It just took your breath away," Gudmestad says.

Down the block from the Shrivers, the Garlach family lived at 323 (now 319–323) Baltimore Street, still a private dwelling owned by Garlach descendents. As the Union soldiers retreated through Gettysburg, the Garlachs received an unexpected guest. Brig. Gen. Alexander Schimmelfennig found himself trapped in a dead-end alley with Confederates blocking all the exits, so he climbed over the Garlach's fence and hid in their backyard for the rest of the battle. At one point, Catherine Garlach even brought him food.

Things became more intense closer to Cemetery Hill. For a time, the front lines passed right through the Rupp family's small brick house. Union soldiers on the front porch fired through the house at the Confederates on the back. After the battle, Rupp said, he scooped up minié balls with both hands. "Our house is prety well riddled," he wrote his sister. The Rupps eventually replaced it in 1868 with the current Victorian gingerbread. It's now the Rupp House History Center, a small museum and educational facility run by the Friends of the National Parks at Gettysburg, a nonprofit organization that works closely with the National Park Service to support the battlefield.

On the other side of Baltimore Street, a giant sycamore tree stands near the site of the McCreary house, now gone. Members of Brig. Gen. Harry Hays's brigade, the Louisiana Tigers, used the house as a sharpshooter's post. "The Rebs occupied Mr. McCreary's house, from which they could pick off our men as they pleased," recalled Rupp. "Our sharpshooters found it out, and kept a look out and finely shot one in Mr.

Neoclassical monuments to generals and regiments adorn Cemetery Hill in Gettysburg National Military Park.

McCreary's front room upstairs and killed him on the spot, and also killed two up in Mr. G. Schriver's house, next to Mr. Pierce's." The Confederate killed at McCreary's was Corp. William Pool, who was crouching behind an overturned table. That table, with the hole from the fatal bullet still in it, is on display in the park's visitor center.

Sitting in the middle of the firestorm near Cemetery Hill was a little brick structure now known as the Jennie Wade house, even though Mary Virginia Wade never lived here. During the battle, Georgia Wade McClellen, Jennie's sister, occupied half of this double house. Jennie lived on Breckinridge Street, while her birthplace, a gray clapboard building, still stands at 242 Baltimore Street. During the battle, Jennie came here to tend her sister, who had given birth to a baby boy on June 26. Jennie was baking bread on the morning of July 3 when a sharpshooter's bullet—possibly fired from the Rupp house, the current Farnsworth House—ripped through two doors and into her heart. She was the only civilian killed during the Battle of Gettysburg.

A statue of Jennie stands in front of the building where she died, which is now a museum—with a gift shop, of course. The north door is still pierced by the bullet hole. Inside, the overall impression is of a close and claustrophobic dwelling, tight confines that must have been almost

The house in Gettysburg where civilian Jennie Wade was fatally wounded is now a museum.

unendurable as the fighting raged nearby. In the basement, a wax figure lies beneath a quilt, just as the dead Jennie did after the family moved down here and cowered during the rest of the battle. Afterward, Jennie was buried in the yard.

Prominently displayed inside the house are copies of the "Certificate of Haunting" issued by the Maryland Paranormal Investigation Coalition. Supposedly the spirits of two boys from the orphanage across the street still make their presence felt here. One thing is undeniable, even to the most hardened skeptic: Ghosts are big business in Gettysburg.

Mark Nesbitt has to take some share of the blame—or credit—for that. Nesbitt was a park ranger at Gettysburg in the 1970s when he began collecting ghost stories he heard, and in 1991 he published them in *Ghosts of Gettysburg.* "Once that book came out I started getting phone calls and letters from people, basically saying, 'My neighbors are wrong, I'm not crazy. Here's what happened to me at Gettysburg,'" he says. "So the tales kept coming in from people." Nesbitt, who has published six books in the *Ghosts* series, plus a *Ghost Hunters' Field Guide,* started offering the tours in 1994.

There's nothing ghostly about Nesbitt, a portly, affable man with a soup-strainer mustache who claims—all evidence to the contrary—that he is a skeptic when it comes to the paranormal. "You have to look at things with a little bit of a jaundiced eye," he says. "Is this really happening?" Still, if there are ghosts, Gettysburg would seem to be a natural spot for them to congregate. "Traditionally a violent, sudden death is what many people believe causes spirits to remain, or be stuck, to where the mortal body perished," says Nesbitt, and Gettysburg had violent deaths in abundance. Visitors have reported seeing apparitions of dead soldiers in Devil's Den, an atmospheric warren of huge, jumbled boulders at the base of Little Round Top. Other people have reported phantoms in Gettysburg College's Pennsylvania Hall, which served as a battlefield hospital. According to one story, when college personnel took an elevator to the basement, the doors opened to show them a horrible scene of Civil War doctors at work and phantom orderlies disposing severed limbs.

"In some of the other paranormal situations I've studied, whenever there's an outpouring of human emotions, there seems to be something we give off," says Nesbitt. "That may be captured somehow in the environment." Now scores of visitors try to find out for themselves by taking all sorts of ghost tours, so many that the borough has to warn tour groups to remain within reasonable sizes and to stay off private property.

If there are any ghosts in Gettysburg, they might be in Evergreen Cemetery, the place that gave Cemetery Hill its name. The Rupps are buried here. So is John Burns, and Jennie Wade was reburied here in 1865. It was a central point on the battlefield, and the cemetery's brick gatehouse—still standing, although with a post-war addition on one side—became a familiar landmark during the battle and in photographs afterward.

The gatehouse was also the home of the Thorn family. Peter Thorn began serving as the caretaker for Evergreen Cemetery in 1856, earning $150 a year. In 1862 he joined the Union army. Peter was with his unit in Washington, D.C., when war reached Gettysburg, and his wife Elizabeth was living in the gatehouse with her parents and her three sons. She was six months pregnant.

When the ill-fated XI Corps came reeling back to Cemetery Hill on July 1, Elizabeth baked bread for the soldiers. Later, she volunteered to show a Union officer the lay of the land, despite the danger from Confederate bullets, and she served a meal to Generals Howard, Sickles, and Slocum. Howard returned the favor by sending over some men to help Elizabeth place her best things in the cellar. "I guess you call all *best*," he said with a smile. "Some I call better than others," Elizabeth snapped.

That afternoon seventeen people crammed into the gatehouse cellar and endured a frightful artillery barrage. After several hours, the door flew open and a soldier stood there. "This family is commanded by General Howard to leave this house and get as far in ten minutes as possible. Take nothing up but the children and go." Go they did, enduring a frightful journey amid bursting shells down a road jammed with milling soldiers and wagons.

After a sleepless night at a nearby farm, Elizabeth and her father went back to the gatehouse to check on their hogs and belongings. Neither had fared well. The hogs were gone, and wounded soldiers in the basement had made short work of the "best things." "The poor wounded men were crying and going on so that we did not want anything then," Elizabeth recalled. "They called their wives and children to come and wet their tongues."

Elizabeth didn't return home again until July 7. "When we looked at the house I could only say 'O my!,'" she wrote. "There were no window glass in the whole house. Some of the frames were knock out and the pump was broken. Fifteen soldiers were buried beside the pump shed." Then the pregnant woman and her father began digging graves. By the time she was done, she had buried more than one hundred soldiers in Evergreen Cemetery. (When her baby was born, Elizabeth named her Rose Meade, after the victor at Gettysburg.) A bronze statue of Elizabeth, a shovel under one arm as she rubs her pregnant belly, the other hand thrown wearily across her brow, stands to one side of the gatehouse she called home.

Robert E. Lee reached the battlefield on July 1 and set up his headquarters in a small stone building on the Chambersburg Pike owned by Widow Mary Thompson. Congressman Thaddeus Stevens, who practiced law in Gettysburg before the war, had acquired the house for her at an auction in 1846. The house still stands, although it was gutted by fire in 1896 and must have been substantially redone inside, and it's now a small museum at the Quality Inn. It has a table and chair that Lee had used when he was here, and some original shutters and siding from a shed outside that had been pierced by bullets. There are also the carbines and revolvers and other weaponry you can expect in a Civil War

Lee set up his Gettysburg headquarters in Widow Thompson's house on the Chambersburg Pike.

A small house near Cemetery Ridge served as the headquarters for General Meade.

museum, as well as the saddle Reynolds was using when the fatal bullet hit him—although the Museum of the Civil War and Underground Railroad in Philadelphia claims to have the real saddle, and a private collector owns a third one.

Meade reached the battlefield in the early hours of July 2. He had been in command of the Army of the Potomac for only four days, yet already he faced the same situation that had brought down his predecessors—a battle with Robert E. Lee. Maj. Gen. Carl Schurz, a Prussian who had a division in the German-dominated XI Corps, recorded that the commanding general had "nothing of pose, nothing stagey about him. His mind was evidently absorbed by a hard problem. But this simple, cold, serious soldier with his business-like air did inspire confidence." After surveying the immediate terrain, Meade set up his headquarters in a little white farmhouse that had just been vacated by a widow named Leister. The house is by Taneytown Road, east of Cemetery Ridge, a tiny, unassuming structure.

Meade's army had suffered a major setback, but it had retreated to a strong defensive position. The Union occupied a fishhook-shaped line that ran from the hook's point at Culp's Hill, around the curve of Cemetery Hill, and south down Cemetery Ridge toward two hills called the

Round Tops. The situation could have been worse. On the first day of battle, Lee had ordered General Ewell to attack the Union position on Cemetery Hill "if practicable." Ewell, his men exhausted and the daylight fading, decided it wasn't.

The Confederates also made attempts to take Culp's Hill, a woodsy rise to the east of Cemetery Hill. Today this is one of the least visited parts of the battlefield, although its woods and rocky terrain create an evocative sense of the 1860s. It also conjures a fascinating human-interest story from Gettysburg.

John Wesley Culp and William Culp were brothers from town who were related to the family that gave Culp's Hill its name. William Culp joined the Union army, but his brother had relocated to Virginia and opted for the Confederacy. The Culp brothers fought on opposite sides at Winchester at the start of Lee's move north. After the battle there, John Wesley reportedly found Jack Skelly, a former friend from Gettysburg who was dying from a wound he received fighting for the Union. Skelly gave Culp a message to deliver to a girl back home—Jennie Wade.

John Wesley ended up fighting on Culp's Hill, a place he knew well from his childhood. It would be fascinating to know what he thought about returning to his native soil as part of an invading army, but we never will. John Wesley Culp died on Culp's Hill. His body was never recovered, and the message he carried for Jennie Wade was lost with him.

Culp's Hill was on the opposite end of the Union line from the Round Tops, which became a focus for battle on July 2. Lee gave the responsibility for attacking the Union's left flank there to Longstreet's I Corps. Longstreet argued for moving the army south to get between Meade and Washington, D.C., but Lee remained adamant that he would fight the battle here. Longstreet's critics have charged that the sulky general then took too long to get his divisions into position, and ended up launching his attack too late in the day. In any event, when Longstreet's men were finally ready to advance, they were surprised to find blue-clad soldiers right in front of them. They belonged to Maj. Gen. Daniel Sickles's III Corps, and they weren't supposed to be there.

Sickles was one of the Union's colorful characters. A Democrat to the core, he was a veteran of the rough and tumble political climate of New York City's Tammany Hall, and had served in London as first secretary to the ambassador, James Buchanan. Sickles was elected to Congress in 1856, and he created a national scandal three years later when he shot

and killed his wife's lover—the son of "Star Spangled Banner" author Francis Scott Key—in Washington's Lafayette Square, just across from the White House. For his defense, Sickles hired Edwin Stanton, who would later replace Simon Cameron as Lincoln's secretary of war. Sickles got off with a verdict of temporary insanity, and then scandalized society again by taking his wife back.

When war came, Sickles raised the Excelsior Brigade in New York and fought bravely on the Peninsula, and as commander of the Army of the Potomac's III Corps at Chancellorsville. But bravery didn't necessarily mean he had good battlefield instincts, and Sickles's actions on Gettysburg's second day aroused controversy. Meade wanted the III Corps positioned near the end of the Union line along Cemetery Ridge just north of the Round Tops. Sickles, on his own initiative, moved his men forward to high ground near the Emmittsburg Road. By doing so, he put them in an exposed position with his flanks open to attack. Meade, who disliked Sickles in the first place, rode over to see what the general was doing. Sickles offered to move his men back, but Meade said it was too late. "You can't hold this position, but the enemy will not let you get away without a fight," he said.

Meade was right. Sickles's III Corps soon found itself in the middle of hell on the second day, as Longstreet's divisions launched attacks that led to savage fighting in the Wheatfield and the Peach Orchard and Devil's Den. Some historians blame Sickles for nearly losing the battle because of his advanced and exposed position. Sickles, however, always maintained that his move had won the day for Meade.

He wasn't around to see the result. Even today you can see a very prominent hole a cannonball punched through the brick barn of the Trostle Farm, below the Peach Orchard. In a field next to the barn, a small monument marks the spot where another cannonball nearly took off Sickles's leg. The general left the battlefield on a stretcher. In true Sickles form, though, he insisted on sitting up and smoking a cigar, so his men would see he was alive and not panic.

Surgeons amputated the leg, which later went on display at the National Museum of Health and Medicine in Washington, D.C. Sickles visited it often. He also settled scores with Meade by attacking his commander via anonymous newspaper articles and by testifying to Congress's Committee on the Conduct of the War that Meade had intended to retreat from Gettysburg after the battle's first day. Despite Sickles's backbiting, Meade remained in command of the Army of the Potomac until the end of the war.

The monument to Sickles's original Excelsior Brigade, near the Peach Orchard on Sickles Avenue, is, not surprisingly, controversial. Sickles headed the commission to raise money for it, but an audit discovered a shortage of $28,000. At the age of ninety-three, shortly before he attended ceremonies at Gettysburg marking the battle's 50th anniversary, Sickles was arrested. Supposedly, his bust was intended to adorn the monument's center, but the funding scandal put the kibosh on that. In fact, Sickles still has no statute on the battlefield.

If Sickles almost lost Gettysburg on the battlefield, he helped save it in Washington. In 1895, a congressman again, Sickles introduced the bill that made Gettysburg a national battlefield. He lived to the ripe old, and often scandalous, age of ninety-four, dying in 1914.

Sickles's move forward left the Round Tops open until Brig. Gen. Gouverneur K. Warren, the Army of the Potomac's chief engineer, reached Little Round Top, realized its importance, and called for troops. His timely action saved this vital spot for the Union, and his statue stands here still, field glasses clutched in one hand as he gazes off in the distance.

Warren helped save the Union army at Gettysburg, but he ended the war in disgrace. Warren, wrote historian Stephen Sears, "neither looked nor acted the part of a warrior general. He was slender and slight of build, and his dark complexion, piercing black eyes, and long straight black hair gave him, people thought, a little of the appearance of an Indian. In manner, however, he was more the fussy Yankee schoolmaster, cautious, fidgety over details, often mean-spirited with subordinates, insistent on doing everything himself so that it would be done properly." After Gettysburg, he was promoted to major general and placed in command of the army's V Corps, even though he persistently irritated Meade by his slowness on the battlefield and his apparent inability to accept orders without quibbling. On April 1, 1865, the fussy Warren collided with the explosive Maj. Gen. Philip Sheridan, to whom Meade had assigned Warren's corps. An aggressive fighter who took no quarter, on the battlefield or off, Sheridan thought Warren had been too slow to support him at the Battle of Five Forks. Even as the war was winding down, Sheridan removed Warren from command and sent him to the rear. For the rest of his life—he died in 1882—Warren fought to have the blot removed from his record. "I die a disgraced soldier," he said on his deathbed.

Warren remains a hero on Little Round Top. In answer to his frantic summons, a brigade under Pennsylvania's aggressively sideburned Col. Strong Vincent arrived just in time with four regiments. They lined up on the Union's left flank, with the 20th Maine, under former Bowdoin College professor Col. Joshua Chamberlain, on the extreme left. Vincent told Chamberlain to hold his position "at all hazards." Chamberlain did, finally routing attacking Alabamians with a bayonet charge down the hill. Thirty years later, widely recognized as "The Hero of Little Round Top," Chamberlain received the Medal of Honor.

Chamberlain didn't win glory in isolation. Brig. Gen. Stephen Weed also made a timely arrival with his brigade and helped shore up the defenses on Little Round Top. Weed suffered a mortal wound. Carried back to the rear, he was left at the farmhouse of Jacob Weikert—where fifteen-year-old Tillie Pierce had gone after fleeing her parents' house on Baltimore Street. Tillie helped comfort the wounded general, but didn't learn his identity until after he died. Weikert's modest stone farmhouse still stands on Taneytown Road, its barn home to Tillie's Treasures Antiques.

Fighting all along the line was fast and furious. Vincent was mortally wounded. So was Col. Patrick O'Rorke. Warren had found O'Rorke, commander of the 140th New York, and ordered him to hurry up Little Round Top. "Down this way, boys!" shouted O'Rorke, waving his sword and urging his men forward at the summit, until a bullet struck him in the neck. O'Rorke's visage appears on the memorial to the 140th New York atop Little Round Top. Thousands of hands have polished his nose to a bright sheen.

Nearby, a miniature castle serves as the monument to the 44th New York. Inside, bronze tablets salute Empire Staters Daniel Butterfield (Meade's chief of staff and the man credited with composing the bugle call "Taps") and Francis Channing Barlow. Barlow was severely wounded on the first day of the battle at the spot now called as Barlow's Knoll. Brig. Gen. John Gordon, who had earlier commanded the Confederate troops at Wrightsville, helped care for Barlow on the battlefield.

Little Round Top is one of the most popular stops at the battlefield, as it should be for scenic value alone. The rocky outcrop provides wonderful views of the rolling fields, from the tumbled boulders of Devil's Den just below. The now-peaceful landscape at the base of Little Round Top, around Plum Run, witnessed so much death and destruction in 1863 that soldiers called it the Valley of Death.

To the north, the Union line stretched across the flat land where the domed Pennsylvania Memorial now stands, past the Copse of Trees that marked the Confederates' high-water mark on the battle's third day, and along up Cemetery Ridge towards the current visitor's center on Cemetery Hill.

Near the Pennsylvania Memorial is another monument of note. The statue atop it shows a soldier making toward the front at double-quick, musket at the ready, and it marks the spot where the 1st Minnesota made a valiant stand against the Confederates, and helped save the battle.

Sickles's move forward left a large gap at this spot. Maj. Gen. Winfield Scott Hancock, commander of the II Corps and one of Meade's most indispensable men, rode up and noticed the Confederates advancing.

He was appalled to see that only the 1st Minnesota was available to plug the gap. "My God! Are these all the men we have here?" Hancock asked. Yet he didn't hesitate to send the outnumbered regiment, a mere 262 men, forward. "Advance, colonel, and take those colors," he ordered, pointing to an enemy flag in the distance. The 1st Minnesota's Col. William Colville and his men advanced at double-quick—just as the figure on their memorial is doing—and delayed the Confederate advance long enough for other Union soldiers to arrive. The 1st Minnesota suffered eighty-two percent

Called "Hancock the Superb," Maj. Gen. Winfield Scott Hancock provided vital service at Gettysburg before being wounded.
LIBRARY OF CONGRESS

Maj. Gen. George Pickett commanded only three of the eleven divisions under Longstreet on July 3, but Lee's final assault is remembered as Pickett's Charge. MILITARY HISTORY INSTITUTE

causalities, Colville among them. Badly wounded, he was nursed back to health at the home of Tillie Pierce and her family.

It had been a close thing at times, but by the end of the second day the Union forces held their positions. That night, Meade held a meeting with his officers in the tiny white house by Taneytown Road and asked their opinions on what the army should do. The responses were unanimous. The army should stay essentially where it was and wait for Lee to attack.

Lee had gone after both ends of the Union position without success. On day three he went after the center, in an attack that has gone down in history as Pickett's Charge. Historians quibble with that designation. Maj. Gen. George Pickett commanded only three of the eleven brigades involved. More accurately, the attack should be known as Longstreet's Assault, after the general whom Lee placed in overall command. Longstreet, who believed the charge was doomed and argued against it with Lee, would not have approved.

George Pickett is another of the Confederacy's flamboyant characters. Like Custer, Pickett had graduated last from his West Point class. A severe wound at the Battle of Gaines's Mill during the Seven Days' Battles outside Richmond had curtailed his fighting. He was a bit of a dandy. One contemporary said he "found the general's hair in long ringlets, hanging below shoulder length and highly perfumed; his beard was likewise curling and giving out the scents of Araby." At Gettysburg, Pickett commanded three brigades, under Gens. James L. Kemper, Lewis A. Armistead, and Richard B. Garnett.

"For every Southern boy fourteen years old, not once but whenever he wants it, there is the instant when it's still not yet two o'clock on that July afternoon in 1863," wrote novelist William Faulkner, when the fate of Lee's army still hangs in the balance and everything is possible:

"Maybe this time," Faulkner wrote. Maybe this time the desperate gamble will pay off.

One hundred and forty-three years later, the reenactors' Confederate banners disappear in the distance as an even larger crowd gathers near the Virginia Memorial. They wear jeans and T-shirts, baseball caps and sneakers, but they're here for the same purpose as the men and women in the hot wool uniforms. They want to walk in the footsteps of Pickett's men on the anniversary of Lee's final assault. Several hundred people have come, so many that park rangers divide them up into three groups, each representing a single regiment in Brig. Gen. Richard Garnett's brigade of Pickett's division.

Gettysburg National Military Park historian Scott Hartwig takes the group that will follow the footsteps of the 19th Virginia. Rangers Rick Bartol and John Heiser take the 8th and 56th Virginia. "You're going to be Confederate soldiers," Hartwig tells the somewhat motley band. "This is the participatory part of the program, and it's what you'll remember long after you've forgotten everything we've told you."

The three groups move out into the field—not along the neatly mowed path that leads directly from the Virginia Memorial to Cemetery Ridge, but out into the tall grass further south, the actual spot where Garnett's brigade would have been. It is hot, almost as hot as it was in 1863, but today's regiments don't have to wait for hours in the hot sun for the order to move, and they don't have to suffer through the massive artillery bombardment that preceded the charge. Nor do they have to face the hostile fire of cannon, rifles, and muskets as they make their way across the field.

On July 3, 1863, this quiet farmland became a valley of blood. The defending fire was deadly. Union artillery commander Henry Hunt had ordered his cannon to stop firing during the Confederate barrage, fooling the Rebels into thinking they had knocked out the Federal guns. In fact, the Confederate cannon had been surprisingly ineffective, their shells soaring over the Union lines. Once the mile-long line of Rebels began moving across the fields toward Cemetery Ridge, the Federal artillery sprang back to life and cut great swathes through the approaching enemy. As the Confederates marched closer, musket fire exploded in great sheets of flame and smoke. The din was terrific, horrific, the firing terrifying. After the battle, a total of 836 musket ball hits were found

Three Confederate prisoners at Gettysburg. LIBRARY OF CONGRESS

in one sixteen-foot-long, fourteen-inch-wide plank from a fence near Emmitsburg Road.

The Park Service has erected similar split-rail fences on the battle-field, and Hartwig's group clambers over some of them and crosses the Emmittsburg Road. Hartwig has the group finish their charge at double-quick, jogging through the weeds and grasses and up the slight rise that leads to the Copse of Trees, the Confederacy's "high-water mark."

A few men of the 19th Virginia made it about this far before being driven back by the Union soldiers who waited here behind a stone wall. Some of the defenders, Hartwig says, had as many as twelve weapons with them, taken from their fallen comrades and pre-loaded. Spectacular as it was, Pickett's Charge ended in failure. The defeated survivors began streaming back across the fields they had crossed at such great cost. Lee rode out to meet them. "It is all my fault," he said.

"Every time I walk that Pickett's Charge, I get two feelings," says Wayne Motts. "I'm sad and depressed, and the second one is I'm proud. I'm proud to be an American. It's not about being right or wrong, it's not about being North or South, it's not about being blue or gray, it's about being an American. That's what it's about. No matter what side you stood on, it's about believing that commitment is worth fighting for."

On July 4, Robert E. Lee began his retreat, a logistically difficult maneuver to move his shattered army back to Virginia. The Gettysburg he left behind was a wasteland, filled with the wounded and the stench of the dead. All available buildings were pressed into service as hospitals, including the County Courthouse and the town's churches. "The sights and sounds at the Court House for a week after the battle were too horrible to describe," said resident Fannie Buehley, who lived across the street.

Mary McAllister lived across from the Christ Lutheran Church on Chambersburg Street. When the church was turned into a hospital, McAllister went over to help. "They carried the wounded in there as fast as they could," she remembered. "Every pew was full; some sitting, some lying, some leaning on others. They cut off legs and arms and threw them out of the windows." On

David Wills spearheaded the creation of the National Cemetery. ADAMS COUNTY HISTORICAL SOCIETY

Abraham Lincoln stayed overnight at the Wills House and added the finishing touches to the speech he gave the next day to dedicate the National Cemetery.
ADAMS COUNTY HISTORICAL SOCIETY

the morning of July 4, Mary heard the sound of a Union band playing, and she said, "I think I never heard anything sweeter, and I never felt so glad in my life."

Around 10,000 people had been killed or mortally wounded during the battle. Governor Andrew Curtin appointed local lawyer David Wills as the agent to deal with the Union dead. Curtin also wrote to the governors of all the Union states to get their agreement to bury their dead in a National Cemetery at Gettysburg. Today the cemetery contains 3,512 bodies from the battle, 979 of them unidentified, in its seventeen acres (plus a five-acre annex). Nine Confederate soldiers are also here, buried among the Union dead by accident.

When Wayne Motts gives tours here, he highlights personal stories that bring the dead men here briefly back to life, at least in his listeners' imaginations. He tells of Captain Nathan Messick of Company G of the 1st Minnesota, the first Federal unit sworn in to fight the war. Messick was killed

President Abraham Lincoln was not even the featured speaker at Gettysburg, but his short speech is the one people remember. LIBRARY OF CONGRESS

by an artillery shell on July 3 during Pickett's charge. Motts points out the stone of George Nixon, great-grandfather of President Richard Nixon, from Ohio. The father of nine children, forty-year-old Nixon joined Company B of the 73rd Ohio. He was a skirmisher at Gettysburg and was shot far in advance of the Union lines on July 2. Richard Enderlin earned a Medal of Honor when he crawled out to Nixon and dragged him back from the front lines at considerable risk to his own life. Nixon died anyway.

The burials were still continuing when Abraham Lincoln came to Gettysburg to make a few appropriate remarks on November 19, 1863. He wasn't the main speaker—that honor belonged to former Harvard president Edward Everett—but it's Lincoln's brief speech that we remember today as the Gettysburg Address. "Many visitors know that Lincoln made a Gettysburg Address before they know there was a battle at Gettysburg," says Motts.

If Lincoln had a real Gettysburg address, it would have to be the Wills House, where he stayed on the night before the ceremony. The large, square building is on the town's main square, but it's currently closed for major renovations. A statue of Lincoln stands on the sidewalk in front of it, in earnest conversation with another statue in modern dress. The pair, the work of sculptor J. Seward Johnson, are called *Return Visit.* Johnson used casts of the president's hands made in 1860 by Leonard Volk and Clark Mills's 1865 Lincoln life mask to create the president, and outlines of Lincoln's shoes made by his bootmaker to get the feet just right.

On the morning of November 19, Lincoln exited the Wills House. The ceremonial procession stepped off around eleven o'clock and made its slow way down Baltimore Street, then onto the Emmitsburg and Taneytown roads to the cemetery entrance. Some 15,000 people showed up for the event, giving Gettysburg an almost carnival aspect.

The speaker's platform was located near where the tall Soldiers and Sailors Monument stands today, not on the site of the current rostrum. Gathered on the platform were Lincoln and Everett, Secretary of State Seward, Governor Curtin, and other notables. Also present was Georgia Wade McClellan, Jennie Wade's sister. Lincoln had specifically requested her presence. She later said she wished she could have slipped away during Everett's two-hour speech.

In comparison to Everett's stem-winder, Lincoln delivered a brief yet eloquent speech that generations of schoolchildren have since been forced to memorize. Even Everett—who opposed Lincoln in the 1860 election as the vice-presidential candidate for the Constitutional Union Party—admitted he had been outclassed. He later wrote that Lincoln had made his point better in two minutes than he had in two hours.

After making his speech, Lincoln returned to the Wills House for a reception, where he asked to see John Burns. "God bless you, old man," Lincoln told him. The president then walked arm and arm with Burns for a ceremony at the Presbyterian Church on Baltimore and High streets. "The President was a tall man and Mr. Burns a small man and as they came along I was amused," a resident wrote. "Lincoln took enormous strides and Mr. Burns could not take strides like that. He could not keep step with the President." After the ceremony, Lincoln boarded a train at the Gettysburg station just north of the square on Carlisle Street (the station's still standing and has been recently restored) for the long ride back to the Washington.

Lincoln still speaks at Gettysburg each November. Jim Getty has been portraying the sixteenth president for three decades now, and each year he takes the speaker's platform at the National Ceremony and recites the Gettysburg Address. The modern Lincoln is not nearly as tall as the real president was, but as you watch and listen to this folksy, craggy-visaged man in his nineteenth-century frock coat and trademark beard, you can think that this is probably what it was like to hear Abraham Lincoln speak.

Getty was a high-school choral director in Ohio in the mid-1970s when he grew a beard. "People started commenting on the Lincolnesque look," he says. Hal Holbrook was doing a one-man show as Mark Twain at the time, and that got Getty to thinking that maybe he could do the same kind of thing for Lincoln. "As my enthusiasm for the idea grew, I

Gettysburg

You can find the **Gettysburg Convention and Visitor Bureau**, 102 Carlisle St., just south of the main square, opposite the train station. (717) 334-6274 or (800) 337-5015, www.gettysburgcvb.org.

Gettysburg National Military Park is operated by the National Park Service. The current visitor center (whose days are numbered) includes a museum and gift shop, and the Electric Map. It's also the place to stop for a battlefield brochure that outlines driving tours and walking tours. Throughout the day, ranger-guided tours depart from various spots throughout the battlefield; you can pick up a schedule at the visitor center. The visitor center is open daily from 8 AM to 5 PM, with expanded hours during the summer season. (717) 334-1124, www.nps.gov/gett. The **National Cemetery** is right across the road from the visitor center and is open from dawn until sunset. The park service also operates the **Eisenhower National Historic Site**, the home of President Dwight D. Eisenhower and his wife, Mamie. The Eisenhowers bought the place in 1950, and they moved here permanently after Ike's last term as president ended in 1960. The farm is accessible to visitors only by shuttle buses that run from the visitor center, with depature times varying seasonally. There is an admission charge. (717) 338-9114, www.nps.gov/eise.

The **Shriver House Museum**, 309 Baltimore St., has been restored to its appearance from the 1860s. There are half-hour tours every hour on the half hour. It is open Monday through Saturday from 10 AM to 5 PM and Sunday noon to 5 PM, from April through November, and weekends from noon to 5 PM in December, February, and March. The house is closed in January. Admission is charged. (717) 337-2800, www.shriverhouse.org.

The **Rupp House History Center**, 451 Baltimore St., has a small museum that focuses on what the battle was like for the civilians. During the summer season, hours are Monday through Thursday noon to 6 PM, Friday noon to 8 PM, Saturday 10 AM to 8 PM and Sunday noon to 5 PM. Reduced days and hours during the off-season. There is no admission fee. (717) 334-7292, www.friendsofgettysburg.org.

You can still see the bullet hole in the doors, and the dough tray Jennie Wade was using at the **Jennie Wade House**, 200 Steinwehr Ave. It's open in season daily from 9 AM to 9 PM, and from 9 AM to 5 PM during the rest of the year. (717) 334-4100, www.gettysburgbattlefieldtours.com/Wade.html. There is an admission charge.

Forget those grainy, 16-mm movies you see at National Park visitor centers. *Fields of Freedom* is big-budget, big-volume film that plays on a huge, three-story screen at the Gateway Theaters just off U.S. Route 15 at the intersection of York Road (Route 30) outside Gettysburg. The thirty-minute film focuses on two soldiers, Union and Confederate, and their experiences during Pickett's Charge, and it provides a good, visceral sense of the battle. (717) 334-5575 or 334-5577, www.gatewaygettysburg.com.

The **Adams County Historical Society** has its headquarters in the old Lutheran Seminary main building. "For anyone interested in researching any aspect of this county, including the Civil War, this is the place that you would want to stop," says its executive director, Wayne Motts. The society's collections include 4,200 cubic feet of paper records, 20,000 objects, and two negative collections with 100,000 photos. It's open to researchers (for a fee) on Tuesday, Wednesday, and Saturday from 9 AM to noon and 1 PM to 4 PM, and Thursday 6 PM to 9 PM. Museum tours are by appointment only. (717) 334-4723, www.achs-pa.org.

Got ghosts? Gettysburg thinks it does and a number of companies will help you find them. The first was Mark Nesbitt's **Ghosts of Gettysburg**, 271 Baltimore St. (717) 337-0445, www.ghostsofgettysburg.com. The **Farnsworth House**, 401 Baltimore St., claims to be "one of the most haunted inns in America" and offers a Civil War Mourning Theatre and Candlelight Ghost Walks. (717) 334-8838. **Sleepy Hollow of Gettysburg Candlelight Ghost Tours** leave from two locations, 65 Steinwehr Ave. and Lee's Headquarters. (717) 337-9322, www.sleepyhollowofgettysburg.com. **Ghostly Images Tours** take their customers to the Jennie Wade House. (717) 334-6296, www.gettysburgbattlefieldtours.com/Ghost.html. If you think ghosts are no laughing matter, think again. The Journey Shoppe, 341 Baltimore St., offers the **Gettysburg Comedy Ghost Tour**. (717) 334-5829, www.gettysburg comedyghosttour.com.

convinced my wife that we should move here," he says, here being Gettysburg, a town that had been founded by a man with a similar name, James Gettys. The Gettys moved in 1977. Now Getty appears as Lincoln at all sorts of programs. He talks about "Lincoln on Leadership" for corporations. He has provided the narration for Aaron Copland's "Lincoln Portrait" at appearances with the Buffalo Philharmonic and the Cleveland Pops, and he appears on the Delta Steamboat Company's Civil War cruises. On November 19, Getty always appears at the National Cemetery to deliver the Gettysburg Address just as the real Lincoln did.

Like William Faulkner said, the past isn't dead. In Gettysburg, it's not even past.

East Cavalry Field

Pickett's Charge took place at Gettysburg on the last day of the battle, July 3, but even as Lee was preparing this final, last-ditch assault on the Federal front, another pitched fight was taking place on a portion of the battlefield that relatively few people visit.

The East Cavalry Field has changed little since Union and Confederate cavalry battled here in 1863. It lies about four miles from the vistor center, west on U.S. Route 30, past U.S. Route 15 and then a right turn onto Cavalry Field Road. A few monuments and markers dot the landscape, but this remains largely unspoiled farmland, open fields that would still make a grand setting for a cavalry charge.

On July 3, Stuart attempted to attack Meade's lines from behind. With him were the men he had taken throughout Pennsylvania, but they were exhausted and reduced in numbers to about 3,000. Stuart also had Albert Jenkins's brigade, although Jenkins himself had received a head wound on the second day at Gettysburg and was out of action.

Stuart's opponents here were some 3,250 Union cavalry under Brig. Gen. David M. Gregg—first cousin to Pennsylvania governor Andrew Curtin. Playing a prominent part in the battle was George Armstrong Custer, who had attached himself to Gregg's division even though he served beneath Judson Kilpatrick. (Kilpatrick was not pleased, but there was little he could do about it.) Fighting began here between artillery and dismounted horsemen in the vicinity of a farm owned by the Rummel family. (The buildings are there still.) Then the Confederate brigades of Brig. Gens. Wade Hampton and Fitzhugh Lee advanced across the fields. "A grander spectacle than their advance has rarely been beheld," wrote Capt. William Miller of the 3rd Pennsylvania Cavalry—whose belongings are on display at the Cumberland Historical Society in Carlisle. "They marched with well-aligned fronts and steady reins. Their polished saber-blades dazzled in the sun." With a shout of "Come on, you wolverines!" Custer—still thirteen years away from his infamous disaster at the Little Big Horn—led a charge of the 1st Michigan Cavalry that helped blunt the Confederate attack.

"As the two columns approached each other the pace of each increased," Miller wrote, "when suddenly a crash, like the falling of timber, betokened the crisis. So sudden and violent was the collision that many of the horses were turned end over end and crushed their riders beneath them. The clashing of sabers, the firing of pistols, the demands for surrender, and cries of the combatants now filled the air." After much savage fighting, the Union forces forced Stuart and his Confederates back. The attempt to attack Meade's rear had failed.

Monterey Pass

Once the Union threw back Pickett's Charge, Robert E. Lee knew he had to get his battered army out of Pennsylvania. The retreat required monumental feats of logistics and planning. The army needed ambulances for the wounded and wagons for the tons of provisions it had foraged. The wagon train for Richard Ewell's division alone stretched for forty miles. Supplying his army from Pennsylvania's riches had been one of Lee's primary goals, after all, and he wasn't about to leave his spoils behind. Making the retreat even more difficult was the driving rain that began on July 4 and turned roads to mud and drenched the defeated army as it made is way back towards the Potomac River and safety.

The quickest way back to the ford across the Potomac at Williamsport, Maryland, was via Fairfield, then across South Mountain at Monterey Pass. Through the downpour of July 4, one of the two southern wagon trains (the other was proceeding via Cashtown Pass) was laboring up South Mountain on a steep, narrow route called the Maria Furnace Road. Heading up the Emmitsburg/Waynesboro Turnpike from the south, on a collision course with the retreating rebels, was Judson Kilpatrick and his Union cavalry.

Visit Monterey Pass today, and you'll find few traces of what happened here. There's only a single historical marker, on the corner of Route 16 and Chariman Road. Traces exist of the Maria Furnace Road, but they're on private property. But lately, with the help of a local group called One Mountain Foundation, and the success of Kent Masterson Brown's book *Retreat from Gettysburg*, interest has been growing about the events at Monterey Pass. One blustery Saturday afternoon in the spring, a crowd of around one hundred people gathered to hear Gettysburg ranger Michael Vallone talk about the battle and explore the ground where it took place.

Kilpatrick's men approached the pass through a pitch-black night, with visibility made even worse by the driving rain. The cavalrymen literally couldn't see their hands in front of their faces until sudden bolts of lightning lit everything for brief instants. On their way up the steep pike toward Monterey Pass, Kilpatrick's men met twelve-year-old Hetty Zeilinger. "What is this twelve-year-old girl doing wandering down the road in the middle of the night?" Vallone wonders. "Did her parents know where she was? Well, times were different then." The girl offered to guide the Union cavalry up to the pass, so one of the Union troopers hoisted her onto his horse.

"She told them, there are Confederates and cannon everywhere," Vallone says. In fact, there were only about ninety men and a single cannon ahead, a short distance before the pike intersected the wagon train as it groaned its way along the Maria Furnace Road. Near the top of the road, at Monterey Pass, Kilpatrick's men, with Brig. Gen. George Armstrong Custer in the lead, ran headlong into this tiny force of defenders, under the command of Capt. George Emack of Company B, 1st Maryland Cavalry. Aided by the darkness and confusion, Emack's small force managed to delay the 4,500 Federal cavalrymen, before they were forced slowly back toward the wagon train. "Incredible bravery," says Vallone. "Incredible action. Brave men."

With the sounds of the wagon train coming from the darkness in front of him, Custer sent the 6th Michigan forward through the dark and rain to attack it. It was so dark, in fact, that one of the dismounted cavarlymen literally stepped on a Confederate lying on the ground in his path, who shot him dead. In the charge that followed, Custer's men captured 300 wagons and 1,300 prisoners during a nightmarish encounter amid crashing thunder and lightning, panicked animals, and screams and shouts. Captain Emack suffered a series of serious wounds before his men carried him to safety.

Henry J. Chritzman of Greencastle, a surgeon with one of the Union cavalry brigades, recalled the scene. "When we came up with the wagon-train, Federal and Confederate cavalry, wagons, ambulances, drivers and mules became a confused mass of pursued and pursuing demons whose shouts and carbine shots, mingled with the lightning's red glare and the thunder's crash, made it appear as if we were in the infernal regions," he wrote. Panicked animals went tearing down the road and plunged over the steep edge, where the wagons crashed to pieces. When Kilpatrick burned his captured wagons later that night, the light from their flames was visible for miles.

Off the Trail

Philadelphia

Philadelphia was spared from fighting during the Civil War, but the city played an important role nonetheless. Philadelphia had a large free-black population and before the war served as an important station on the Underground Railroad. During the war, Philadelphia contributed 100,000 soldiers, and not a few generals, to the Union cause. George Gordon Meade, commander at Gettysburg, was from Philadelphia (although he had been born in Spain), as was George McClellan.

The Civil War and Underground Railroad Museum of Philadelphia is certainly one of Pennsylvania's more eclectic museums, and the world's oldest Civil War museum. It dates back to 1888 and its founding by members of the veterans group MOLLUS, the Military Order of the Loyal Legion of the United States. These veterans had gathered their memorabilia from the war, and in 1922 moved the collection to this four-story rowhouse on Pine Street. For years it was known simply as the Civil War Library and Museum, but in 2003 it expanded its mission to include the Underground Railroad.

There are even more fundamental changes in store, starting with a change in location. By 2009 the whole collection—3,000 artifacts, 7,000 books, and thousands of photographs and documents—will move to a building leased from the National Park Service at Independence Mall. Hopefully, the change won't obliterate the museum's unique personality. Visiting it is like stopping at the house of an eccentric Civil War collector, complete with creaking stairways and worn wooden floors. It's stuffed with all sorts of memorabilia, including relics related to Abraham Lincoln, Ulysses S. Grant, and Jefferson Davis. Staring lifelessly from a glass case on the first floor is the head of Old Baldy, General Meade's horse. The horse outlived the General, and died in 1882 at the age of thirty.

You can find Meade himself at Philadelphia's Laurel Hill Cemetery, the final resting places of forty Civil War generals. The hillsides in this necropolis above the Schuylkill River are a riot of Victorian funerary sculpture, including carved wreaths, broken columns, weeping figures, urns, shields, angels, and obelisks by the score. Meade and his family reside beneath modest stones and a very large maple, on the slope of a hillside overlooking the river.

Airplanes come sweeping in low over Fort Mifflin, which bills itself as "the fort that saved America." In 1777 this bastion on the Delaware River delayed a British fleet attempting to resupply the Redcoats who hoped to crush George Washington's army. Repaired and refurbished during the Civil War, the fort housed prisoners—Confederates and Union military as well as civilian political prisoners guilty of everything from

George G. Meade and forty other Civil War generals rest in Laurel Hill Cemetery in Philadelphia.

Philadelphia

The Civil War and Underground Railroad Museum is at 1805 Pine St. and open Thursday through Saturday 11 AM to 4:30 PM and other days by appointment. There is an admission charge. The museum also has story hours on alternate Saturdays, and occasional living history programs. The museum offers discounted parking at the parkway lot on the corner of 17th and Pine sts. (215) 735-8196, www.cwarmuseum.org.

Laurel Hill Cemetery at 3822 Ridge Ave. is open weekdays from 8 AM to 4:30 PM and weekends from 9:30 AM to 5 PM. There is no admission charge. (215) 228-8200, www.thelaurelhillcemetery.org.

Fort Mifflin on Fort Mifflin Road is open April through November, Wednesday through Sunday from 10 AM to 4 PM. There is an admission fee. (215) 685-4167, www.fortmifflin.com.

The Civil War History Consortium is a group of twenty-two institutions in the Philadelphia area with links to the war. You can get a complete listing of its member organizations, plus links to their websites, at www.civilwar consortium.org.

Fort Mifflin served as a prison during the Civil War.

murder to "disloyal language." Today the fort is a city historic site. It's a little tumble-down, but still a great place to explore. Since it's just below a flight path for Philadelphia International Airport, visitors can react with awe to the jetliners passing overhead.

Pittsburgh

Like Philadelphia, Pittsburgh was spared from fighting, but not from participating in the Civil War. When the North remained unsure of Robert E. Lee's plans in June 1863, rumors said that Pittsburgh was his goal, and some citizens began erecting street barriers. It turned out to be a false alarm, of course, but to better defend the western part of the state the government created the Department of the Monongahela and placed it under the command of Maj. Gen. William T. H. Brooks, who established his headquarters in Pittsburgh.

The Allegheny Arsenal in nearby Lawrenceville played a very important role during the war. One of its primary manufactures was cartridges, and in 1862 an explosion there killed seventy-eight workers, the war's worst civilian tragedy. The site of the arsenal is now Arsenal Park, behind a middle school. The victims, only fifty-four of whom could be identified, were buried in Allegheny Cemetery, 4734 Butler Street. Pittsburgh's Fort Pitt Foundry was also vital to the Union cause, turning out 2 million cannon and 5,000 tons of shot.

The Soldiers and Sailors Memorial Hall was originally conceived by members of the Grand Army of the Republic to commemorate the Civil War veterans from Allegheny County. In the years since, its mission has

 Pittsburgh

The **Soldiers and Sailors Memorial Hall**, 4141 Fifth Ave., is open Monday through Saturday from 10 AM to 4 PM. There is an admission charge. (412) 621-4253, www.soldiersandsailorshall.org.

The **Senator John Heinz Pittsburgh Regional History Center**, 1212 Smallman St., is open daily from 10 AM to 5 PM. There is an admission charge. The library and archives are open Tuesday through Saturday from 10 AM to 5 PM. (412) 545-6000, www.pghhistory.org.

expanded to include veterans from all the country's wars. The state's second largest military museum (Gettysburg being the first), the memorial has artifacts—uniforms, equipment and other items—as well as copious records and manuscripts, including information compiled from Grand Army of the Republic posts.

The Soldiers' Monument near the aviary was originally sculpted by P.C. Reniers and erected in 1871. It's been relocated and its beaux-arts pedestal removed in 1931.

For a wider view of Pittsburgh's history, visit the Senator John Heinz Pittsburgh Regional History Center, which operates in a restored 1898 ice house. Expanded in 2004 in partnership with the Smithsonian Institution, the center now includes a Western Pennsylvania Sports Museum, an education center, and a special collections gallery. Its 200,000 square feet of exhibits covers 250 years of western Pennsylvania history.

Bibliography

Alexander, Ted. *History and Tour Guide of the Burning of Chambersburg and McCausland's Raid.* Columbus, OH: Blue & Gray Enterprises, 2004.

Ayers, Edward L. *In the Presence of Mine Enemies: War in the Heart of America, 1859–1863.* New York: W. W. Norton, 2003.

Baker, Jean H. *James Buchanan.* New York: Times Books, 2004.

Borit, Gabor S., ed. *The Gettysburg Nobody Knows.* New York: Oxford University Press, 1997.

Brown, Kent Masterson. *Retreat from Gettysburg: Lee, Logistic, and the Pennsylvania Campaign.* Chapel Hill: University of North Carolina Press, 2005.

Brunhouse, Robert. *Miniatures of Mechanicsburg.* 1928; reprint, Mechanicsburg, PA: Mechanicsburg Museum Association, 1986.

Burg, Steven B., ed. *Black History of Shippensburg, Pennsylvania: 1860–1936.* Shippensburg, PA: Shippensburg University Press, 2005.

Burkhart, William, et al. *Shippensburg in the Civil War.* Shippensburg, PA: Shippensburg Historical Society, 1964.

Civic Club of Carlisle, Pennsylvania. *Carlisle Old and New: 100th Anniversary Edition.* Harrisburg, PA: J. Horace McFarland, 1973. Originally published in 1907.

Conklin, Eileen F. *Women at Gettysburg, 1863.* Gettysburg, PA: Thomas Publications, 1993.

Conrad, W. P., and Ted Alexander. *War Passed This Way.* Shippensburg, PA: Beidel Printing House, Inc., 1982.

Crist, Robert Grant. *Confederate Invasion of the West Shore—1863.* Lemoyne, PA: Lemoyne Trust, 1963.

_____. *Camp Hill: A History*. Camp Hill, PA: Plank's Suburban Press, 1984.

Early, Jubal Anderson. *War Memoirs*. 1912; reprint, Bloomington, IN: Indiana University Press, 1960.

Faust, Patricia L., ed. *Historical Times Illustrated Encyclopedia of the Civil War*. New York: HarperCollins, 1986.

Fisher, Samuel L. *The Burning of Chambersburg*. Philadelphia: Reformed Church Publication Board, 1879.

Foote, Shelby. *The Civil War: A Narrative*. New York: Vintage Books, 1986.

Gettysburg Expedition Guide. Narrated by Wayne Motts. Bedford, NH: TravelBrains, Inc., 2000. Sound recording.

Gordon, John B. *Reminiscences of the Civil War*. New York: Charles Scribner's Sons, 1903.

Hamilton Library and Historical Association of Cumberland County. *Two Hundred Years in Cumberland County*. Carlisle, PA: Hamilton Library and Historical Association of Cumberland County, 1951.

Hatch, Carl E., Richard E. Kohler, and John F. Rauhauser Jr. *Essays on York, Pa. History, 1776–1976: A Bicentennial Commemorative*. York, PA: Strine Publishing, 1976.

Historical Publication Committee of the Hanover Chamber of Commerce. *Prelude to Gettysburg: Encounter at Hanover*. Shippensburg, PA: Burd Street Press, 1962.

Hoch, Bradley R. *The Lincoln Trail in Pennsylvania: A History and Guide*. University Park: Pennsylvania State University Press, 2001.

Johnson, Robert Underwood, and Clarence Clough Buel, eds. *Battles and Leaders of the Civil War*. New Jersey: Castle, 1982.

Keefer, Norman D. *A History of Mechanicsburg and the Surrounding Area*. Mechanicsburg, PA: Mechanicsburg Area Historical Committee, 1976.

Keener-Farley, Lawrence E., and James E. Schmick. *Civil War Harrisburg: A Guide to Capital Area Sites, Incidents and Personalities*. Rev. ed. Harrisburg, PA: Camp Curtin Historical Society, 2006.

Keneally, Thomas. *American Scoundrel: The Life of the Notorious Civil War General Dan Sickles*. New York: Doubleday, 2002.

McClellan, H. B. *The Life and Campaigns of Major-General J. E. B. Stuart, Commander of the Cavalry of the Army of Northern Virginia*. 1885; reprint, Secaucus, NJ: Blue & Grey Press, 1993.

McClure, Alexander K. *Old Time Notes of Pennsylvania: A Connected and Chronological Record of the Commercial, Industrial and Educational Advancement of Pennsylvania, and the Inner History of All Political Movements Since the Adoption of the Constitution of 1838.* Philadelphia: John C. Winston, 1905.

McClure, James. *East of Gettysburg: A Gray Shadow Crosses York County, PA.* York, PA: York Daily Record, 2003.

McPherson, James. *Battle Cry of Freedom: The Civil War Era.* New York: Oxford University Press, 1988.

_____. *Hallowed Ground: A Walk at Gettysburg.* New York: Crown Publishers, 2003.

Miller, William J. *The Training of an Army: Camp Curtin and the North's Civil War.* Shippensburg, PA: White Mane Publishing, 1990.

Nesbitt, Mark. *Ghosts of Gettysburg: Spirits, Apparitions, and Haunted Places of the Battlefield.* Vols. 1–5. Gettysburg, PA: Thomas Publications, 1991–2000.

_____. *Saber and Scapegoat: J. E. B. Stuart and the Gettysburg Controversy.* Mechanicsburg, PA: Stackpole Books, 1994.

Nye, Wilbur Sturtevant. *Here Come the Rebels!* Baton Rouge: Louisiana State University Press, 1965.

Sears, Stephen W. *Gettysburg.* Boston: Houghton Mifflin, 2003.

_____. *Controversies and Commanders: Dispatches from the Army of the Potomac.* Boston: Houghton Mifflin, 1999

Small, Cindy L. *The Jennie Wade Story: A True and Complete Account of the Only Civilian Killed During the Battle of Gettysburg.* Gettysburg, PA: Thomas Publications, 1991.

Stackpole, Edward J. *They Met at Gettysburg.* Harrisburg, PA: Stackpole, 1956.

Stern, Stephen Z. *The Union Cavalry in the Civil War, Vol 1: From Fort Sumter to Gettysburg.* Baton Rouge: Louisiana State University Press, 1979.

Stiles, Robert. *Four Years Under Marse Robert.* New York: Neal Publishing, 1903.

Thompson, John W. *General J. E. B. Stuart's Raid Through Mercersburg.* Mercersburg, PA: Mercersburg Printing, 1999.

_____. *Horses, Hostages, and Apple Cider: J. E. B. Stuart's 1862 Pennsylvania Raid.* Mercersburg, PA: Mercersburg Printing, 2002.

Wert, Jeffry T. *Custer: The Controversial Life of George Armstrong Custer.* New York: Simon & Schuster, 1996.

Wheeler, Richard. *Witness to Gettysburg.* New York: Meridian, 1987.

Women's Club of Mercersburg, Pennsylvania. *Old Mercersburg.* 1912; reprint, Williamsport, PA: Grit Publishing, 1949.

Acknowledgments

This book would not have been possible without the work of the many great writers who came before me. I am standing on the shoulders of giants and am particularly indebted to Wilbur Nye's *Here Come the Rebels!*, an informed and entertaining account of Lee's Pennsylvania campaign, and W. P. Conrad and Ted Alexander's *War Passed This Way.*

I would also like to thank all the people who shared their time, knowledge, and books with me. The list includes Merri Lou Schaumann at the Cumberland County Visitors Bureau; Mike Perry at the U.S. Army Heritage and Education Center; Jim Schmick of Civil War and More in Mechanicsburg; the staff at the Cumberland County Historical Society; John Fenstermacher, who was kind enough to show me around the Rupp House; James W. Thompson IV and Tim Rockwell in Mercersburg; Stacey Fox at the Gettysburg Convention and Visitors Bureau; Bob Hill at the Historical Society of Dauphin County; Calobe Jackson Jr.; Harrisburg mayor Stephen R. Reed; Brett Kelley at The National Civil War Museum; Bonnie Shockey at the Allison-Antrim Museum; Dr. Stephen Burg of Shippensburg University; Nancie Gudmestad of the Shriver House Museum; Jim Getty; Terri Durden; Mark Nesbitt; Dr. John Rumm of the Civil War and Underground Railroad Museum of Philadelphia; and Jason Miller at the Civil War Flag Conservation Facility. Donna Schorr of the Greater Philadelphia Tourism Marketing Corporation arranged lodgings for me in that great city, for which I thank her.

I'd like to thank Wayne Motts of the Adams County Historical Society. He was kind enough to meet with me and share his copious knowledge of Gettysburg. He also read over the Gettysburg chapter and saved me from making a number of embarrassing mistakes, and he dug into the Society's archives to provide photographs. Richard Saylor and Michael O'Malley of the Pennsylvania Historical and Museum Commission also read over the manuscript, and their corrections make me seem much more knowledgeable than I would have without their help. Thanks also to Lenwood Sloan, Director of Heritage Tourism in the Pennsylvania Tourism Office, for his support throughout this project.

Thanks also to Tony May, Pete Shelly, and Elizabeth Gray at Triad Strategies, who provided me lots of Civil War-related work that helped keep me afloat as I was writing this book. Some of the material here originated with research I did for them.

My editor at Stackpole Books, Kyle Weaver, was unfailingly patient and helpful throughout the process, and this book wouldn't have been possible without him. And of course my family—my lovely and talented wife Beth Ann and my two children, Katie and Sam—provided plenty of support as I worked on this. Beth Ann, especially, is always a pillar of strength and a fount of wisdom at those times I'm ready to toss the keyboard out the window. Her encouragement and love keep me going.

Index